WATER FROM
SAND RIVERS

WATER FROM SAND RIVERS

Guidelines for abstraction

Stephen W. Hussey

Water, Engineering and Development Centre
Loughborough University
2007

WEDC

Water, Engineering and Development Centre
The John Pickford Building
Loughborough University
Leicestershire
LE11 3TU
UK

t: +44 (0) 1509 222885   f: +44 (0) 1509 211079
e: wedc@lboro.ac.uk   http://www.lboro.ac.uk/wedc/

Hussey, S.W. (2007)
Water From Sand Rivers: Guidelines for abstraction
WEDC, Loughborough University, UK.

ISBN Paperback 978 1 84380 126 9
ISBN Ebook: 9781788533683
Book DOI: http://dx.doi.org/10.3362/9781788533683

Produced in association with
Dabane Trust, Zimbabwe and WETT, UK

Dabane Trust

WETT

Designed by Rod Shaw and Kay Davey
Illustrations by Ken Chatterton
Cover painting by Rod Shaw

This edition is reprinted and distributed by Practical Action Publishing.

Since 1974, Practical Action Publishing has published and disseminated books and information in support of international development work throughout the world. Practical Action Publishing trades only in support of its parent charity objectives and any profits are covenanted back to Practical Action (Charity Reg. No. 247257, Group VAT Registration No. 880 9924 76).

The cover illustration represents a sand-abstraction pump
under development with Dabane Trust

All photographs were taken by the author unless otherwise stated.

Please note: The views expressed in this publication are not necessarily those of
WEDC, Loughborough University

About the author

Stephen Hussey is the Director of Dabane Trust and has been involved with the development of basic methods of water storage and sand-abstraction for more than 30 years. He has undertaken an extensive research and development programme to demonstrate the benefits of the water resource that is held in sand river aquifers in dryland marginal areas. This work ultimately led to the award of Ph.D. from Loughborough University. In the course of both his work and research a number of simple methods of sand-abstraction have been developed. In this book he shares his experience and ideas in the hope that they will inspire development workers in dryland areas to review their water supplies and to consider alternative, low-cost options.

Dabane Trust

Dabane Trust is a non-governmental organization based in Zimbabwe. It has been developing basic forms of sand-abstraction for use by rural communities since 1990 and has installed more than 100 simple abstraction systems to provide clean water for household use and for small-scale irrigation and livestock water schemes. The basic technology is a simple and sustainable method of water abstraction that can be operated and managed by rural communities with low technical capabilities. Systems sited in areas where the nutritional status is low have been providing surrounding communities with vast quantities of fresh vegetables and have been in independent operation for over 15 years.

WETT

The Sustainable Water Extraction Technology Trust (WETT) is a British registered charity which supports the development of low-cost, sustainable water supply programmes. Their particular focus is remote dryland areas where the strategy is to assist rural communities to upgrade their traditional water supplies and install, operate and manage this themselves. WETT is interested in identifying interested organizations and in training personnel in the development of alternative water supply systems. It is also involved in research activities which will identify potential water supply locations and lead to wider usage of sustainable small-scale water supply systems.

Acknowledgements

I am most grateful to the assistance provided by WEDC staff, especially Bob Elson, Rod Shaw, Kay Davey and Tricia Jackson and to Ken Chatterton for the production of many of the illustrations. Thanks must also go to the trustees and staff of Dabane Trust especially Melusi Mafu, Florence Ndlovu, Thelma Ntini, Thembalani Tshuma, Douglas Nleya and Ekron Nyoni. The book is sponsored jointly by Dabane Trust and WETT and has been funded by Action for World Solidarity (AWS), Tudor Trust and the Department for International Development (DFID).

My most sincere thanks go to my family, Inez Hussey, Juliet Campbell, Joseph Hussey and Colin Campbell for their input, their encouragement and their patience; and also to Richard Cansdale, Richard Knottenbelt, Frances Chinemana and Tom Hill.

I also thank Eric Nissen-Petersen of ASAL Consultants Ltd, Nairobi, Kenya, for the references to hydro-dynamic wells he has pioneered; ALIN – Arid Lands Information Network-Eastern Africa, Nairobi, Kenya, for the use of the cartoon featured on page 124 and to Johnson Screens for their representation of a naturally developed sand filter featured on page 39; to FAO Publications for Table 7.1; to Brian Skinner of WEDC for use of the sand dam diagram featured on page 58; to World Water – Faversham House Group for the data contained in Table 7.3 and to Vernon Gibberd for his contribution on hafirs.

Foreword

The scene for this book can be drawn from amaNdebele folklore describing the traditional belief of the people of the semi-arid area of western Zimbabwe.

In the very beginning the World was dry, flat and featureless – devoid of life. God was not at all impressed, so he decided to send his Son to Earth. He gave him a bow and arrow and told him that if he wanted to call God, he should stamp on the ground.

At first the Son did not know what to do in this arid, barren World. He then remembered God's instruction, to stamp on the earth. He looked around for something to stamp on and finally, after much searching, he found a small stone – a tiny pebble. He stamped on this and immediately mighty rocks sprang up out of the ground. Thus the Matopo Hills were formed. The skies darkened and a huge cloud formed overhead. The Son was frightened and took his bow and shot an arrow into the cloud. Immediately lightning flashed and torrential rain poured down and cascaded off the rocks. The Son saw that God and the water were one.

The Son then took a needle and sewed the rocks together; the thread formed the rivers that flowed between the rocks. Life started in the valleys and people came. Thus the Son saw that God was the water and the water was the people and that the people were the water and were God.

Through this traditional belief amaNdebele people conceptualize the interdependence of water and religion. The communication with ancestral spirits, with a divine creator and with the all-pervading need for water in an arid and harsh environment are omnipresent.

Throughout the world, water is perhaps the resource most taken for granted. In arid and semi-arid areas, however, this is far from true and providing a family with sufficient clean water can be a formidable task. In dryland areas of Zimbabwe, for example, distances of up to 9 kilometres have been recorded from permanent homes to water-points and in both South Africa and Zimbabwe homes have been recorded at altitudes of up to 500 metres above a reliable water-point. In remote areas of Mozambique, women are known to walk for up to 10 hours in one direction to collect water. To carry a weight of 20 kilograms in such situations is a Herculean task and one that ultimately yields only 20 litres of water, the absolute minimum requirement for just two people.

Even where there is infrastructure to abstract or store water there may well be severe limitations. The systems to maintain or repair pumps are often woefully inadequate resulting in numerous water-points which are non-operational. Water may be too deep to draw using a simple handpump and dams too full of silt to maintain permanent water supplies.

In such situations every conceivable type of water supply must be considered and alternative water supplies, that might at first appear inadequate, need to be reviewed. Sand-abstraction – the abstraction of water from unconsolidated sand aquifers, particularly sand river aquifers – is a basic water supply system that has its origins rooted in traditional practices and can be suitable in many situations. Although it is highly-appreciated and sustainable, the technology has not attracted the attention of the mainstream water development industry even though the materials of the deep groundwater industry are used.

As a result, there is a particular dearth of practical information for project managers and fieldworkers concerning basic, low-level technologies for sand-abstraction. It is this which this book sets out to redress. It provides an overview of the conditions in which sand-abstraction is an option. It enables practical people to understand the technology and the technical and sociological factors required to make it sustainable.

The book is also aimed at providing decision-makers in the water industry, commercial, government and non-governmental organizations with an overview of an alternative, appropriate water supply solution that is particularly suitable for use by poor communities in dryland areas where water is scarce.

Stephen Hussey
Zimbabwe, 2007

Contents

Figures

Photographs

Tables

What is sand-abstraction?

The availability of water in dry areas

Water is a resource that is unevenly distributed throughout the world and is often subject to excessive and disproportionate use. Over time, many areas have developed a water deficit where demand exceeds the possibility of supply. For everyone to live a normal and healthy life, however, there must be an adequate supply of water. Ideally, this should include water for livestock and irrigation. Water for irrigation allows for the small-scale farming of vegetables or protein crops as a supplement to staple foods.

In arid and semi-arid areas (sometimes referred to collectively as dryland areas) the rainfall is often unreliable, typically comprising storms that are intense but of short duration. Often in these dryland areas there is not enough rainfall to ensure that crops can be grown reliably. The period of time between adequate rainfalls can be so long that crops become water-stressed and wilt or die. Where rainfall is low, the rivers may not flow throughout the year. Depending on the geographical location and the rainfall season, river flow may vary from a few weeks or months to just a few hours in a year, or over several years.

Despite limited rainfall in dryland areas, water is generally available in aquifers underground. Depending on the geology, the nature of the rocks

Water is often considered to be both a renewable and an infinite resource – it is neither!

and soil, as well the climate of the area, water may occur at depths from just a few centimetres to several hundred metres. In many arid regions groundwater aquifers have a limited potential or are deep and difficult to access. Deep water aquifers are generally slow to drain and so collect high concentrations of mineral salts from the rock to the extent that the water becomes unpalatable and sometimes unusable. During years of drought in particular, aquifers may be severely depleted and unable to sustain the local community. Water in an aquifer is usually abstracted through boreholes and wells.

Although water can be stored in dams in dryland areas, ideally a dam should have a deep basin so that the water does not have a large surface area exposed for evaporation. In areas where the average ambient temperature is high, water loss is likely to be severe from the open surface water of a dam. Flat areas do not make good dam sites as the water depth in the dam is likely to be limited and the water liable to dry up. In arid areas that are prone to erosion the useful life of a dam may be significantly reduced by excessive deposits of silt within the dam basin.

Small amounts of water can be stored in water harvesting tanks but their effectiveness is often limited, particularly in regions with short and erratic rainfall seasons or where the seasons are long, hot and dry. In these conditions, supplies can deplete quickly and not be frequently replenished.

Within arid areas water is naturally retained in the sediment of sand river channels although in a dry riverbed this is not always apparent. The water in a sand river is clean and not subject to the same amount of evaporation as an open surface dam. Sand river water supplies can be used to augment the supply of water from underground aquifers and dams, especially in remote rural areas where it is imperative that local communities are able to operate independently and maintain their own water supplies. Sand dams and sub-surface dams function like sand rivers as they retain water in the sediment and reduce evaporation.

The system of sand-abstraction

In dryland conditions soils are easily eroded and with occasional but heavy downpours, large quantities of coarse material are washed into the waterways. In situations where sediment builds up, these become the sand rivers and 'wadis'[1] so common in arid areas. These rivers often contain

---

[1] A Wadi is a dry riverbed in an arid zone that contains water only during times of heavy rain. As flow is often the result of an intense localized storm a wadi typically has no source or outlet.

Abstraction
The process of drawing water from an aquifer

Sand-abstraction
The process of drawing water from sand rivers

Photograph 1.1. A resident of Huwana village draws clean water for household use from an open sand-well on the Manzamnyama River, Matabeleland South, Zimbabwe

large volumes of unconsolidated sediment that retains water in the pore spaces. In a large river system the supply of water in the sediment can last all year round. Such water retained within sand riverbeds has been used by arid-land dwellers for centuries and is an established and accepted practice.

New and imaginative initiatives to abstract this water require identification and development. Sustainable water abstraction systems that are acceptable and manageable by rural communities are required to augment existing water supplies.

> Sand-abstraction can provide a source of water in arid and semi-arid areas. In many situations sand river aquifers constitute a viable water resource with significant potential.

Traditional systems make water available through temporary sand wells that are dug in the riverbeds and are regularly deepened as the water-level drops. A shallow film of water is exposed that can be scooped out with a small dish. To increase the depth of water within the well to some 50mm, an open-ended 20 or 100 litre drum is dug into the water-bearing sand (Photograph 1.2). This method of abstraction is low-cost, practical, easily constructed and completely sustainable which makes it popular with poor communities.

Photograph 1.2. A traditional open sand well

These traditional wells are vulnerable however, and only last a season. The sides of the wells are un-shored and unstable so the sand falls slowly down into the bottom and requires cleaning out every time it is used. Often the wells are fenced with brushwood to prevent animals from entering the pit as they increase the movement of sand into the well and foul the water. Brushwood fences, however, are themselves a problem (Photograph 1.3). When the river next flows, the wells fill with brushwood and silt which complicates re-excavation of the well in the following seasons. Over time, trapped brushwood may collect silt and other debris in the river channel creating false islands which further reduces the well site area and may widen or clog the river and cause flooding.

The present technology of sand-abstraction is the result of a progression from the traditional open sand well to the installation of sub-surface abstraction equipment that will effectively separate water from sand. Each system uses a screen to control the movement of sediment so that water becomes free of suspended particles and is accessible for abstraction. Depending on the system, once the water is free of sediment it can be drawn to the surface by anything from a bucket to a mechanically-powered pump. Screens for sand-abstraction come in the form of well-points, infiltration galleries or part of a caisson or well shaft. A particular advantage of a sand-abstraction system is that the water is not open to contamination but is naturally filtered and cleaned.

Photograph 1.3. Brushwood fencing surrounding a traditional sand well

The common use of the term 'sand-abstraction' is unfortunate as it does little to explain or promote the method of water abstraction. A more appropriate term would be 'water-from-sand-abstraction' as the method is that of drawing water from saturated river sediment and not the removal of sediment from sand rivers as the common term might imply.

Freshwater in rivers and lakes together with soil moisture and groundwater accounts for less than 1% of the total volume of the world's water resource.

Chapter summary

Sand-abstraction is a useful water resource that is available to vulnerable communities in harsh dryland areas. It has been used for centuries by remote rural communities and has become an acceptable source of water that many people understand and are able to manage to great advantage. As a means of providing a source of safe water, however, it is a methodology that has not been developed by the water supply industry, nor become a solution adopted by national water supply authorities or development agencies. Sand-abstraction can be a useful, alternative source of water in dryland areas that can be managed and operated independently by low-income communities. It has the potential to augment supplies provided by established water supply systems.

There is a need to further appreciate the potential of sand-abstraction and to understand how to access water in this way. The starting point for this is to understand sand rivers and their potential for storing water, and to understand the system of sand-abstraction.

2

Sand rivers

What are sand rivers?

In arid-land conditions erosion processes are often immature[2] and soils are comprised of coarse-grained particles generally classified as sand. Soil erosion increases where there is bare land or where the surface slope is steep. Where excessive erosion occurs, particles of soil will reach and eventually fill the river channel, possibly to a depth of several metres. Sand rivers, therefore, are literally rivers that are full of sand. In very dry areas sand rivers often have no headwater or outlet. Isolated heavy precipitation causes runoff that rapidly runs into a river channel causing it to flow until the water is absorbed by the sediment. Such rivers are known as 'wadis'.

The formation of a sand river

In arid and semi-arid areas the precipitation is less than the potential evapo-transpiration[3]. The rainfall that does occur is usually erratic and varies from one year to another. An area that might have an annual average precipitation of 350mm may receive less than 300mm a year for several years and then receive over 1000mm. Although temperatures in dryland

---

[2] In this context 'immature' means 'not completely broken down' i.e. — the erosion process has reached a stage where the soils are predominantly sandy. Further breakdown is required in order for the soil to consist of smaller particles that are not as easily eroded.

[3] Evapo-transpiration: the total loss of moisture from the soil and open water through evaporation and by transpiration from growing plants in the form of water vapour.

Photograph 2.1. An aerial view of the Manzamnyama River, a sand river in a dryland area of western Zimbabwe

areas are typically hot they may also range to cold, particularly at night. These extremes, the combination of erratic, but generally low rainfall and typically hot conditions results in little organic matter residing in the soil.

Low rainfall also means that the process of soil formation remains incomplete resulting in sandy soils that do not hold together and are easily washed away. Figure 2.1 (a) and (b) represent the effect of a drop of rain on sandy soil with little organic matter, whilst (c) represents the loosened particles in suspension which are easily moved. In particular, where there is little vegetative cover, soils without organic matter can become compacted and rainfall cannot easily penetrate. In very dry soils the surface tension of water can prevent percolation. The soil is then exposed to the full impact of heavy rain and eventually becomes loosened and carried away by water run-off.

As water moves across the land surface it carries suspended sediment into the waterways; first into runnels, then streams and finally into

(a) Dry compacted surface. The action of the sun has removed almost all moisture and destroyed the organic matter that would have helped to absorb precipiation.

Soil particles are in contact with each other. There is no organic matter to bind soil particles together.

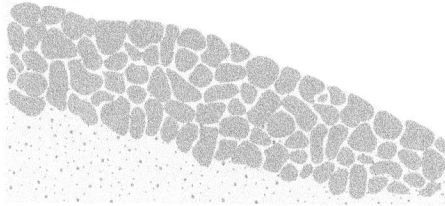

(b) A falling raindrop impacts on the soil surface, it does not penetrate the soil but rebounds and consequently dislodges soil particles.

(c) The soil surface with its loose particles becomes saturated. As precipitation increases so water movement occurs and there is a flow of water and soil particles that will eventually reach a river.

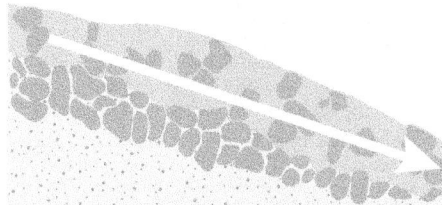

Figure 2.1.   The action of a raindrop on soil with a low organic content

rivers. Depending on the slope of the river, sediment of differing grades is deposited along the length of the river channel. In fast flowing sections of a river with a steep incline only gravel and cobbles are retained and the depth of sediment does not appreciably accrue, frequently remaining at half a metre or less. Rocks and boulders remain in the riverbed as the finer material is swept further downstream. Table 2.1 provides a classification of eroded material by individual grain size, description and discontinuity.

As the slope of the river channel decreases, first gravel then sand and fine sand is deposited along the riverbed, until where the river course levels and the velocity of flow is reduced silt and clay are deposited. It is the slow moving sections of rivers where the slope of the riverbed has levelled that the finer sediment is retained.

Deposits of alluvium[4] are usually not of a uniform particle size throughout their depth. As sediment is transported through the river channel so it becomes 'sorted' with larger, heavier material moving toward the base of the riverbed. Depending on the depth of water that flows through the river channel each season, and the subsequent volume or depth of sediment that is transported and deposited, separate layers of sediment are formed and reformed. Each layer is itself graded and thus bands of alluvium occur from fine to coarse and back to fine again, as shown in Photographs 2.2

Table 2.1. Classification of eroded material by size, description and discontinuity based on BS 5930 (1981)

Grain size	BS 5930 standard	Description	Void space
Rock < 256mm	>2000mm	Boulders	Extremely large
Rock fragment between 256mm and 64mm	2000 - 600mm	Boulders	Very large
	600 - 200mm	Boulders	Very large
	200 - 60mm	Cobbles	Large
Cobble	60 - 20mm	Coarse gravel	Large
Rock fragment between 64mm and 2mm	20 - 6mm	Medium gravel	Moderate
	6 - 2mm	Fine gravel	Moderate
Mineral or rock grains - 2mm – 0.0625mm (often composed of quartz)	2 - 0.6mm	Coarse sand	Small
	0.6 - 0.2mm	Medium sand	Small
	0.2 - 0.06mm	Fine sand	Very small
Sediment with particles	0.06 - 0.02mm	Silt	Very small
Sediment with particles	<0,002mm	Clay	Extremely small

---

[4] Alluvium: soil or sediments deposited by a river or other running water comprising gravel, sand, silt and mud.

Photographs 2.2 and 2.3. Sorting and layering of sediment in river alluvium

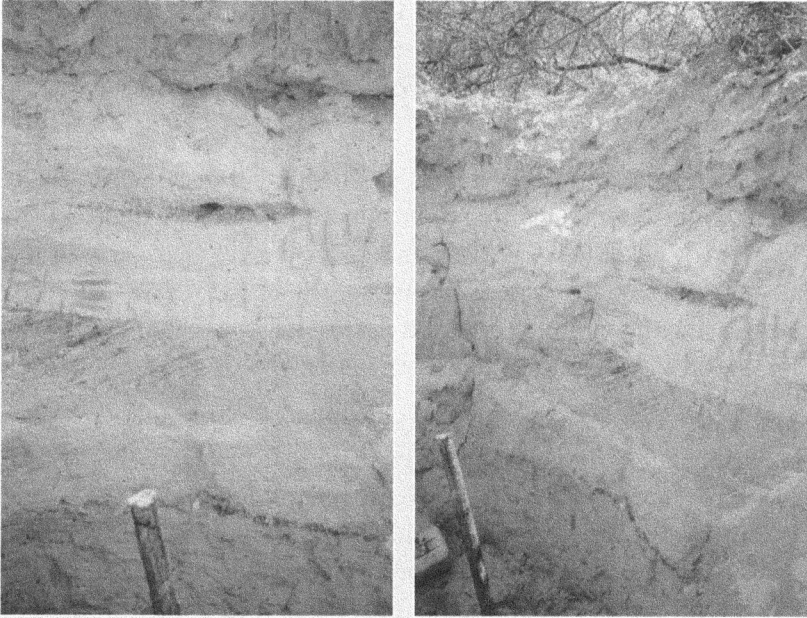

and 2.3, with an overall general increase in particle size with depth. The grade of sediment deposited also depends on the material that is washed into the river channel. In steep hill regions the source material will be large and heavy but in flat areas that are comprised of wind-blown sand the river alluvium will be comprised of smaller and more uniform size 'clasts'[5].

Depending on the conditions and depth of the river channel as the gradient reduces so sediment is retained to a greater depth. At a stage where the slope is reduced to about 1:250, sediment begins to build up in the depressions and undulations of the riverbed and behind natural impediments such as rock outcrops. As more sediment is deposited so a point is reached where there is no further increase in depth. At this stage the amount of sediment deposited equals the amount transported through the river channel. The river is then in equilibrium, with the same depth of sediment being retained from one year to the next. In this condition (provided there is a sufficient depth of sediment) the river channel will have a potential for useful water storage in the river alluvium.

---

[5] Clasts: Clastic sedimentary rocks. Sedimentary rocks are those composed predominantly of broken pieces or 'clasts' of older weathered and eroded rocks.

The incline of the riverbed and the subsequent velocity of flow of the river determines the grade of sediment that is deposited, which then builds up in depressions and behind rock bars and outcrops of the riverbed as shown in Figure 2.2. Sediment is held by underground dykes that prevent the water from progressing downstream. Where water is held in existing natural formations people living downstream are not artificially deprived of water.

Every river and stream that retains sediment will at some time and to some degree hold water within that alluvium. Even small streams that keep water for just a few weeks or only days in a year can be used for the transient reserve of water that occurs following periods of runoff. The more extensive the sediment bed and the greater the recharge, the greater the likelihood of a perennial supply of water.

The amount of water which can be retained in a given volume of sediment can be established through calculating the porosity, which is the ratio of the fraction of pore space or voids to the volume of material of the sediment. The period of water retention within the river channel is dependent on the recharge from rainfall to the river aquifer, the corresponding water-table level and losses from the alluvium. Figure 2.3 indicates the relative position of the groundwater table in a dryland area to the river aquifer in seasons associated with differing rainfall.

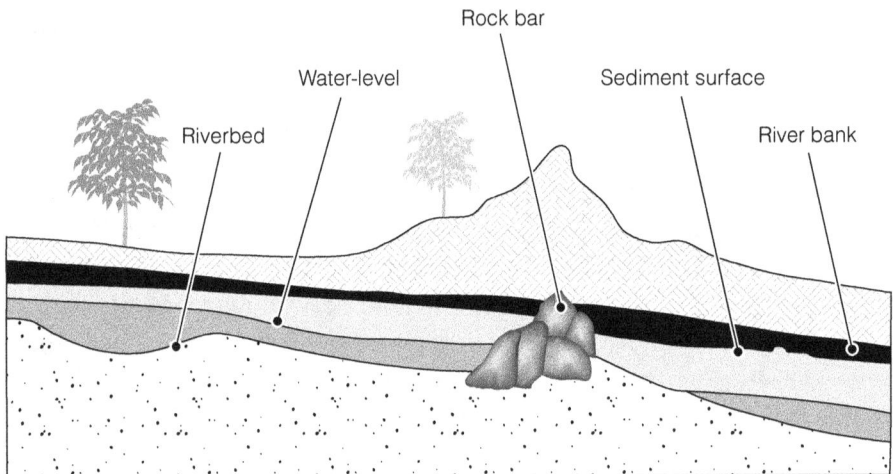

Rock bar

Water-level

Sediment surface

Riverbed

River bank

Figure 2.2.   A section of sand river channel showing sediment retention and water-levels in relation to the riverbed and sediment surface level

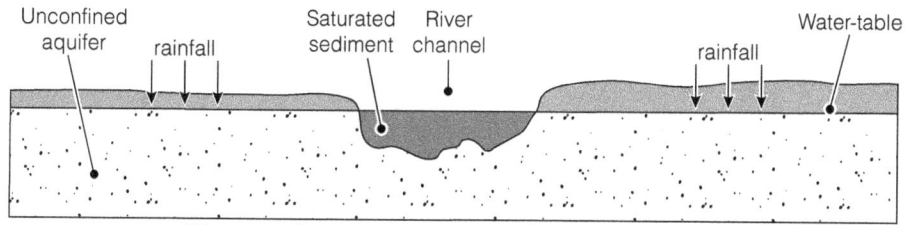

River aquifer in rainy season of adequate rainfall

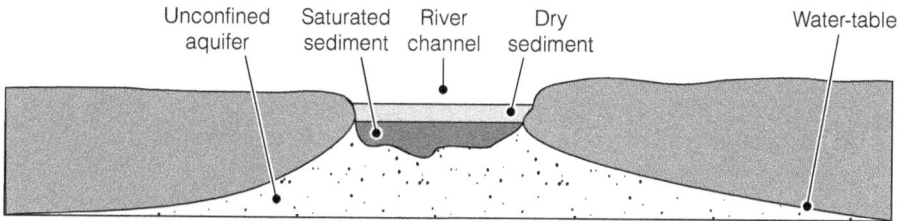

River aquifer in dry season following rainy season of adequate rainfall

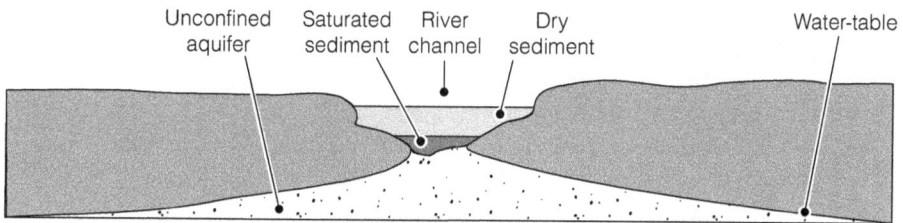

River aquifer in dry season following rainy season of inadequate rainfall

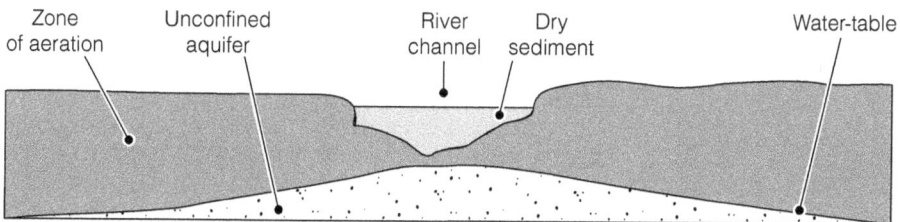

River aquifer in dry season of drought year

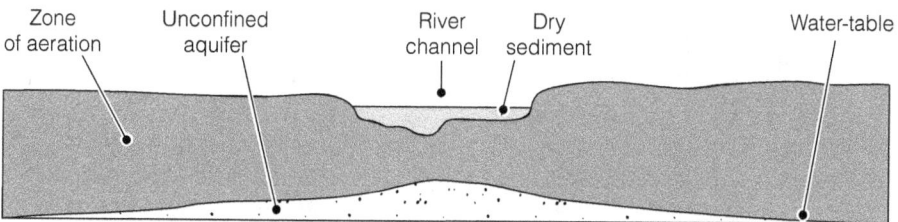

Small river channel in dry season

Figure 2.3.   Unconfined aquifers in wet and dry seasons

Conditions that create a sand river where sand-abstraction can be put into practice

- Prolonged dry seasons with hot ambient temperatures and a potential for evaporation that greatly exceeds precipitation during most of the year.
- Poorly developed unstable soils prone to erosion.
- A low organic matter content of surface soil and low microbial populations within the soil that preclude the percolation of moisture through the soil.
- A limited vegetation canopy with little litter due to a sparse distribution of trees and shrubs. This contributes to soil compaction and the subsequent formation of a seal on the soil surface from the impact of rain drops which reduces permeability and creates overland flow and subsequent erosion of the soil surface over large areas of land.
- A river channel with gentle bends and low banks. A channel with steep sides indicates high rates of flow and high rates of sediment transport with possible damage to abstraction equipment and possibly little sediment retention. A meandering channel indicates slow river flow with possible deposits of fine deep sediment and silt.
- Sections of riverbed with depressions or natural barriers that hold bodies of water and prevent downstream movement.
- A sediment grade of medium sand. Gravel and coarse sand indicate a fast draining aquifer, fine sand and silt indicate low transmissivity and a higher rate of evaporation.

A temporary sand aquifer requires:

sufficient depth of sediment;
coarse deposits; and
extensive bed of sediment.

Ancient river channels

In certain parts of the world the principles of sand-abstraction may be applied in paleo river channels. These are ancient river courses that have been filled with sediment in the same way as present day sand rivers are, but from which the watercourse has subsequently been diverted or where climatic changes have occurred causing the river to stop flowing. The waterway has thus been lost and subsequently may well have been vegetated. The result is an aquifer of unconsolidated alluvium, generally with good water storage characteristics. These sandbeds are particularly prevalent in the Sahel region in areas such as northern Nigeria and western Sudan.

The occurrence of sand rivers

Sand rivers occur in all dryland regions of the world where erosion occurs. They are found, therefore, in the drier regions of many countries in Africa and Asia, as well as Australia and parts of both North and South America. Figure 2.4 shows the major arid areas of the world.

People have always drawn water from these sand rivers but with improved technology it is possible to abstract greater quantities of cleaner water.

Water storage potential of sand rivers

Within a sand river, water is stored in the pore space between the particles of sediment. When the river flows the sediment becomes saturated and if there is sufficient precipitation, flow will occur above the sediment surface. Because of the nature of short, sharp tropical storms the surface water quickly drains through the river channel leaving the riverbed sediment fully saturated. This is now a sand river aquifer at full storage capacity. The potential for water storage differs, however, depending on the river basin and the source material that has been eroded and reached the river channel. Where the deposited material is coarse sand from granite or gneiss, there is good potential for water storage but where it is fine, aeolian sand[6] the potential is considerably reduced.

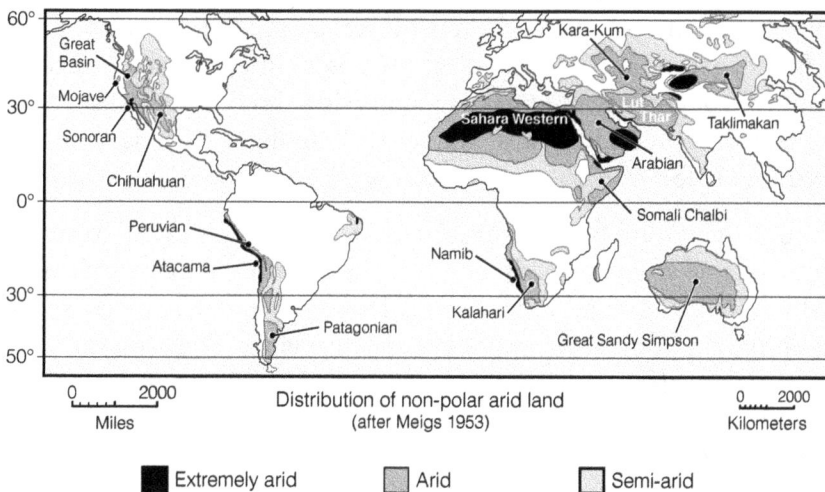

Figure 2.4. United States Geological Survey World Arid Zone Map

---

[6] Aeolian sand: material which has been transported by the wind and as a consequence is worn and deposited as small, rounded particles.

As with all aquifers water retained in the river sediment is subject to losses:

Channel drainage

Even though there is no flow of water in the river above the surface of the sediment, water still continues to drain along the river channel through the sediment, although more slowly.

Evaporation

Evaporation continues from the surface although the deeper the water drops in the sediment the slower the rate of loss. Depending on the grain size and grading of sediment there is very little effect of evaporation below around 900mm.

Percolation/ bed seepage

Seepage occurs into the riverbed and riverbank. The amount depends on the height of the surrounding water-table and on the nature of the riverbed (i.e. whether it is formed of rock or sand.)

Abstraction

This is influenced by the human activity carried out near the river for domestic needs, livestock watering, gardens, brick moulding and other livelihood-based requirements.

Water quality of sand rivers

The quality of water drawn from the deep sediment of sand rivers is often of a remarkably high quality. Typically it may be considered safe for use as a household water supply and almost certainly for use as livestock water and for irrigation and other project purposes. In effect, the percolation of water through river sediment is a huge slow-sand filter system, and as the water does not come into contact with sunlight there is little or no growth of algae.

Although it cannot be guaranteed that all water drawn from sand river sediment is immediately potable, the cleaning process that occurs usually results in a 'safe' water supply. However, where there is excessive contamination of the sediment — for instance where there is a very heavy concentration of livestock fouling the surface beside a drinking point within the river — the process cannot be expected to remove all harmful bacterial.

Table 2.2 shows the low count in a chemical analysis of a sample of water drawn from sediment in the Pohwe River, Gokwe South District, Midlands Province, Zimbabwe.

The water purification process

Water purification through sand river alluvium is a process of mechanical and physical actions that remove unwanted impurities and organic matter and leave them harmlessly within the sediment bed.

Very fine particles and pathogenic organisms that are present in the raw water are removed through a combination of sedimentation, filtration, adsorption and chemical and biological actions.

As contaminated water passes through the sediment bed the larger impurities are deposited and smaller particles are removed by straining. The process continues to the smallest impurities which become attached to individual grains of sediment. Each sediment particle becomes covered with a thin layer of silt, organic material and micro-organisms which in turn adsorb further impurities.

Harmful bacteria are removed by the action of protozoa that also become attached to the sediment grains. Organic matter that is removed by filtration is broken down to carbon dioxide and other oxides by micro-organisms that exist within the sediment bed.

Table 2.2. Chemical analysis of water from a sand-abstraction source

		Standards Association of Zimbabwe. Standard 560:1997		Sample from Pohwe River
		Maximum recommended limit	Maximum allowable limit	
Conductivity	m³/m	70	300	53
pH		6.5 - 8.5	6-9	8.0
Turbidity	NTU	1	5	4.2
Total Hardness	As $CaCO_3$	20 - 300	500	128
Calcium	As $CaCO_3$	150	200	60
Magnesium	Mg	70	100	17
Alkalinity		NS	NS	376
Chlorine	Cl	200	300	2
NS – Standard not specified				

Chapter summary

Conditions that give rise to sand rivers occur in almost all hot dry areas where there are long periods without rainfall. Invariably, in these arid areas there are incomplete weathering processes and little organic matter in the soil so it erodes easily. River channels in these areas fill with coarse sediment that retains water in the pore spaces. The conditions that give rise to sand rivers and the formation and extent of sediment beds in the river channel influences the water reserve and the potential to abstract water. Geological conditions, the local environment and nature of the river channel as well as atmospheric conditions, each have a significant impact on the water retention and loss characteristics of water in a sand river.

Frequently, there are useable quantities of safe water retained in the river alluvium. To maximize the potential of this water resource, the identification of a suitable river is required along with water abstraction sites within a river channel.

3

Site identification
and selection

IN THIS CHAPTER:
- The requirements for sand-abstraction. The conditions and situations in a river where sand-abstraction can be practized
- Site selection – significance of the river catchment area; volume and velocity of flow; river profile, depth, width and length of sediment beds; ideal abstraction points in the river channel; the likelihood of damage to abstraction equipment.
- Sediment analysis – water storage potential, water yield potential.

Selection of a suitable river

Provided there has been some flow within the channel, water will always be retained to some degree in the sediment of a sand river each year. As not all sand rivers have the capacity to retain water all year round, it is necessary to identify those riverbeds that are suitable for sand-abstraction and to select optimum abstraction sites.

Primary factors in the identification of a suitable site:

- **Extent of the river catchment area.** Water flow in a river channel that drains a small catchment area is unlikely to be sufficient to recharge a riverbed aquifer to provide a year-round water supply. Although the river sediment itself may be fully recharged, unless the riverbank and riverbed are also recharged, water loss by infiltration to lower levels from the river channel may quickly deplete the reserve. Variations in annual rainfall within the catchment also have an effect on the recharge to the aquifer. An ideal catchment area is one where immediate runoff is impeded so that over time there is a slow, continuous recharge into the river channel.

- **Size of the river and volume of sediment.** It is necessary for a river channel to be wide enough and deep enough to contain sufficient sediment to retain water all year round. The length of sediment beds between obstructions in the river is also important. If too short and the aquifer too small, the water resource will be over-abstracted or will drain too quickly for a continuous supply. However, where there is an insufficient natural deposit, it is sometimes possible to increase the volume of sediment through the construction of a sand-dam.

- **Gradient of the river.** The velocity of flow through a river channel is important; if it is too fast, as is the case in headwaters, sediment will not be deposited or will be transported through the channel with a depth of disturbance sufficient to damage or dislodge abstraction equipment. As a general rule, where the slope of the riverbed is greater than 1 in 100, not only will there be an insufficient depth of sediment, but water will be lost to rapid drainage through the channel. Where the velocity of flow is exceptionally slow, sediment that is too fine for satisfactory sand-abstraction will be deposited.

- **Characteristics of the sediment.** The water storage potential of a possible abstraction site can be assessed through a number of observations and tests.
  — Fine sediment indicates an aquifer with a small total void space, which in turn provides limited water storage potential.
  — Well-sorted sediment that is primarily comprised of coarse grains with little silt will indicate a site with a suitable water storage potential. Water will flow quickly through sediment that has little 'fines' to the point of abstraction. Cementation — a process where the pores between grains of sediment become in-filled with smaller and smaller grains — indicates a low water storage potential and poor permeability.
  — Sediment that is friable or 'loose' with little cementation, where the packing is natural and not unduly compressed or compacted will have a large percentage void space available for water storage.

Photograph 3.1 shows a stable sand river where the gradient is low and the sediment is in equilibrium. Such a river can be expected to have a large water storage capacity and is suitable for water abstraction through well-points as explained in Chapter 4.

Photograph 3.2 shows an unstable river where the flow is fast and turbulent. When in flow, this river transports large material as can be seen from the number of boulders and cobbles.

Photograph 3.1. Maitengwe River, Matabeleland South, Zimbabwe

Photograph 3.2. Utete River, Mashonaland West, Zimbabwe

Photograph 3.3 shows a small sand river with a limited water storage capacity. Such a small stream may not provide a perennial supply of water.

Physical characteristics of a river

Selection of a suitable site

An ideal site for the installation of a sand-abstraction system is in coarse sediment in a former river pool or on the outside of a river bend in deep sediment in a slow moving river. A suitable site will require identification through surveys of the topography of the river channel. This will require definition of stages of the river channel and points of identification in the river where there is deep sediment or sediment-filled depressions.

To ensure a successful installation:
Identify a site where there is sufficient depth and volume of sediment to maintain a year-round water supply and where the abstraction equipment will not be disturbed by the river flow.

Photograph 3.3. Mahuwe River, Mashonaland West, Zimbabwe

Practical site assessment

- Observe the course of the river and where sediment is retained — sediment will be deeper on the outside of a bend, against the steeper bank in the course of the river or behind a dyke or outcrop of rock on the riverbed.

- Determine the extent of the sediment bed, its width and length. Probe the sediment to determine the greatest depth of sediment. A deep sediment bed indicates a useable reserve of water that is less likely to dry out. The more extensive the sediment bed the greater the volume of water.

- Observe the gradient — the slope of the river sediment surface. A low, gentle slope will indicate a useable length of sandbed with a flow rate through the river channel sufficiently low to prevent damage or wash away of any equipment in the riverbed or on the riverbank.

- Observe and carry out appropriate tests to determine the nature of the sediment. Coarse grained sediment will indicate the possibility of a large storage capacity, fine sediment will indicate a reduced storage and abstraction potential.

REMEMBER

A small river generally indicates a small water supply.

Table 3.1 provides a rough assessment of the suitability of a river for sand-abstraction.

Riverbed profiles

Typically, a sand river is not a continuous length of silted river that is even in its depth or length, but is comprised of a series of sections or reaches of river between obstructions such as rock bars or sub-surface sills or dykes. These break up the river channel into water yielding sections or compartments. Within these reaches there are likely to be natural depressions and undulations that create shallow and deep sections in both the length and width of the river channel. Such conditions occur particularly in the slower flowing and wider reaches of a sand river where there is likely to be a greater potential for sand-abstraction. Deeper sections tend to coincide with the main course of river flow that invariably meanders even within the river channel, particularly when the river flow is not excessive. Identification of deeper sections of river where there will

Table 3.1. Overview of the suitability of a river for sand-abstraction

River characteristic	Site assessment
Large wide river	Probably an ideal site can be identified.
Small, narrow river	Limited volume of sediment, therefore likelihood of limited water retention.
Straight river section – low banks	May be ideal, but may have a limited depth of sediment.
Straight river section – deep banks	Greater depth of sediment to retain water but increased likelihood of abstraction equipment being disturbed or damaged by sediment transport when the river is in flow.
Inside bend	Limited depth of sediment, therefore limited water retention. May require a long length of inlet pipe to reach a satisfactory abstraction point.
Outside bend	Greater depth of sediment but when river flows may be too fast and cause damage or disturbance to abstraction equipment.
Rocky outcrops	May help to retain sediment and thus water upstream. May increase the turbulence and velocity of river flow and thus the likelihood of damage to equipment downstream. May indicate small, disconnected alluvium beds with limited water storage potential.

be an increased volume of water is critical to a successful sand-abstraction installation, particularly in marginal areas.

There is sometimes a possibility of using a site on the inside of a river bend or alongside a river section where the riverbank is alluvial and the well-point can be installed deeper than it could be within the actual river channel. Figure 3.1 indicates preferred locations for abstraction sites within a sand river channel.

Site selection tests

Observations and tests will be required in order to identify potential sites within suitable rivers. For a satisfactory site it will be important to determine the nature of the sediment and to estimate the likelihood of a permanent supply of water. Methods through which this may be achieved are:

- **Local knowledge of the area.** Local people will generally be able to provide an accurate, if only preliminary, assessment of the water supply potential and the permanence of a prospective site.

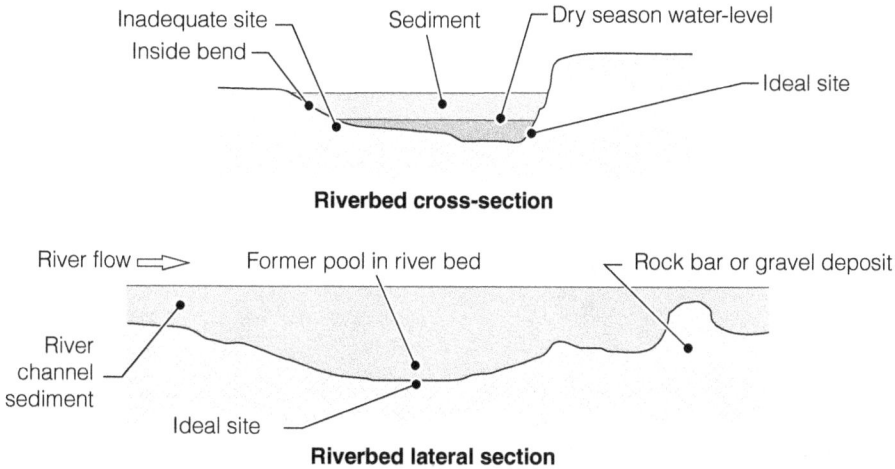

Figure 3.1. Riverbed profiles indicating preferred sites

- **An indication of the water supply potential** may be obtained by observation of riverine vegetation, which will generally be large and possibly verdant where there is a channel aquifer with a plentiful supply of water, as shown in Photograph 3.4.

- **Appraisal of existing open sand wells.** The suitability of a possible site may be gathered through the inspection of any traditional sand wells in the immediate vicinity towards the end of a dry-season. If there are useable quantities of water the scoop wells will generally be in use, but if the water-level has been depleted the wells will be merely dry, sand-filled depressions.

- **Probing the sediment depth** with a pointed steel rod as shown in Photograph 3.5, is a quick and relatively easy method of gauging whether or not water is present below the sediment surface. This can be done by noting the depth of sediment and whether or not there is moisture on the probe on removal from the sediment. By assessing the ease or difficulty required to insert the probe and by observing the particles adhering to the probe, it is also possible to gain an indication of the nature and consistency of the sediment.

- **Excavation.** If there are no existing scoop wells the level of water within the sediment at any one time may be accurately established by digging a temporary well or pit.

- **Identification of water within river sediment** could be established by the ancient practice of water-dowsing. Although it may be possible to

Photograph 3.4. Riverine vegetation indicating good water potential

Photograph 3.5. Establishing the depth of sediment with a probe

identify a source of water, however, it is unlikely that reliable data can be obtained on either the depth of sediment or the depth of water.

- **Augering.** Samples of sediment from within the aquifer may be obtained by augering to the river basement. However, the extraction of samples from saturated sediment is difficult without specialist equipment due to fluidization of the sediment.

- **Electromagnetic resistivity.** A technically advanced solution is to undertake a geophysical survey of a proposed site. This has the potential to determine both the water-level and the base of the riverbed. However, such equipment is more generally used to determine fracture zones in deep aquifers and there is the possibility of misinterpretation when attempting to establish the depth and profile of a relatively shallow riverbed. Although it is possible to establish the boundaries of differing materials it is not always possible to determine the actual material and whether or not it is the riverbed base, or merely a gravel layer caused by bedload sorting, within the river channel.

A piezometer tube installed into the riverbed through which the water-level in the river alluvium can be measured will provide a long-term record of the depth of water at any time within the sediment.

POROSITY
The amount of water that is contained within the sediment

SPECIFIC YIELD
The amount of water that can be abstracted from an aquifer —
in this case the river sediment

PERMEABILITY
The rate at which water is able to pass through sediment

VOID RATIO
The ratio of the fraction of voids to the volume of total particles
in which they occur

Systematic in-field assessment of a sand-abstraction site

A series of observations and tests may be conducted on-site for a quick assessment of a possible abstraction site. Although specialist equipment is required to provide any degree of accuracy an indication of the yield potential may be gained through quick, practical, rule-of-thumb tests using basic equipment such as a probe, a sieve and small container, a 50m and a 3m tape measure and a shovel, as shown in Photograph 3.6.

Photograph 3.6. Site assessment equipment

D. Ngwenya

1. Water resource

- *Vegetation* — Prolific and/or massive vegetation will indicate the likelihood of an extensive reservoir of water within the river channel.
- *Volume of sediment bed* — (width length breadth). Measure the width and length with a tape measure or by pacing. Assess the depth by probing with a steel rod to the base of the river channel, marking and measuring the depth of sediment. Accuracy will be increased with the number of probe readings made to provide an average depth of the aquifer.

2. Specific yield

- *Porosity* — The fineness or coarseness of sediment at the proposed site will provide an indication of the void ratio. Run a sample of sediment through the fingers onto a small plastic sheet. Coarse sediment will fall straight down, fine sediment will drop slowly and will be moved by air currents and thus tend to fall away from the main pile. An appraisal of the proportion of coarse to fine sediment will indicate the water storage potential, the finer the sediment the more likely that it will pack together to decrease the void space.
- *Packing* — The size and shape of a sample of sediment grains will provide an indication of the void ratio of the sediment and the potential for water yield. Rub a sample of sediment grains between the palms of the hands to assess the texture through a coarse or smooth feel. Observe the general size of particles, the uniformity of size and the roundness or elongation of grains. The more rounded the grains and the more uniform the size, the greater the void space will be between grains. Sharp or elongated grains indicate a likelihood that the grains will pack together to reduce the total void space.
- *Permeability* — A thorough assessment requires an in-field permeability test. A fair indication may be obtained from the:
  Void space — Check for fines, coarseness and sorting of sediment and for compaction and cementation of the sediment. Excavate a pit in the sediment; note the stability of the sides, the consistency of the material, the layering of sediment deposits and any orientation of sediment grains. The more stable and vertical the sides of the pit the greater the extent of fines and compaction, and consequently, the smaller the void space with reduced permeability.
  Saturation of sediment — Examine the nature of the sediment by digging into the water-bearing sediment. Fluidized sediment indicates a high degree of permeability. Non-fluidized sediment indicates considerable contact between the sediment grains and poor permeability.

3. Water loss from sediment

- *Coarseness of sediment* — fine sediment indicates a greater likelihood of loss through increased capilarity and subsequent evaporation.
- *River gradient* — a steep gradient indicates a greater propensity for downstream drainage than a more level riverbed.
- *Riverbed base* — An unconsolidated riverbed indicates susceptibility to seepage to the underlying water-table. A riverbed with a rock base will indicate a reduced seepage potential. A dense layer of clay on the base of the of the river channel may effectively limit seepage

4. Security of installation

- *High or low energy flows* — A fast flowing river has the potential to damage an installation during periods of peak flow. Observe the riverbed gradient, the depth of the riverbank sides and the occurrence of cobbles on the sediment surface or the sides of the riverbank. A meandering river will not be fast flowing. The depth to which sediment is transported through a river channel increases exponentially, (not just proportionally) with the depth of flowing water and thus increases the likelihood of damage to equipment.
- *Flotsam* — Observe the height to which debris is deposited above the riverbed. The greater the height of water flow above the dry-season sediment surface, the greater the depth of river flow and hence scour below the sediment surface and the greater the risk of damage to the well-point and/or connecting pipes of an installation.

Site yield assessment — physical characteristics of the sediment
Figure 3.2 indicates the comparative water storage potential of coarse, moderate and fine grained sediment.

General indication of water storage potential

- Large grains of sediment with few fine grains indicate a good water storage potential.
- An even distribution of large to fine grains indicates a fair water storage potential.
- Small grains with a lot of fines indicates a limited or poor water storage potential.

Figure 3.2. Indication of water storage potential

Assessing the possible water yield from sediment

Once a site that has a potential for sand-abstraction has been selected it will be advisable to assess the water storage capacity. Determining the water storage capacity and the yield of a site is a science in itself requiring accurate grading of the sediment to determine the range in size of individual grains and the percentage of each size in the sample.

Although it may not be possible to obtain sediment samples from three or more metres deep, or to undertake such accurate grading of sediment, in order to indicate the characteristics of a sample of sediment from a river that is ideal for sand-abstraction a sediment grading analysis is given (see Table 3.2). To determine a sediment grading curve, a sample of riverbed alluvium is passed through a series of six sieves, usually with apertures of 2.00, 1.00, 0.50, 0.25, 0.125 and 0.063mm. The sample is agitated for 10 minutes in a specialist shaker and the resulting data used to plot a logarithmic graph similar to the one shown in Figure 3.3. From the table and graph below it can be seen that 30% or more of the sediment particles in the centre and lower levels are of a dimension of 2.00mm or more at their narrowest point which is ideal for a well-point sand-abstraction system. Less complex methods of assessing sediment suitability are discussed later in the chapter.

Specialist equipment is also required to achieve a degree of accuracy in determining the porosity and permeability of a sample of sediment. However assessed, porosity is a calculation of the void space of the sediment and thus the pore space that is available for water storage and permeability is a measure of the rate of flow through a sample.

Table 3.2. Grading curve of sediment obtained from the upper, centre and lower levels of the Manzamnyama River at Huwana, Matabeleland South, Zimbabwe

Sieve (mm)	Upper sample (gms)	% retained	% passing	Centre sample (gms)	% retained	% passing	Lower sample (gms)	% retained	% passing
5	0.0	0.0	100.0	0.0	0.0	100.0	0.0	0.0	100.0
2	119.7	17.4	82.6	255.3	33.6	66.4	270.0	30.5	69.5
1	285.5	41.6	41.0	286.2	37.6	28.8	730.8	48.7	20.9
0.5	180.4	26.3	14.7	147.0	19.3	9.5	140.5	15.9	5.0
0.25	62.0	9.0	5.7	40.3	5.3	4.2	27.2	3.1	1.9
0.125	21.2	3.1	2.8	12.4	1.6	2.6	10.9	1.2	0.7
0.063	14.9	2.2	0.4	14.9	2.0	0.6	4.0	0.5	0.2
Base	3.0	0.4	0.0	4.7	0.6	0.0	2.1	0.2	0.0
Total	**686.7**			**760.8**			**885.5**		

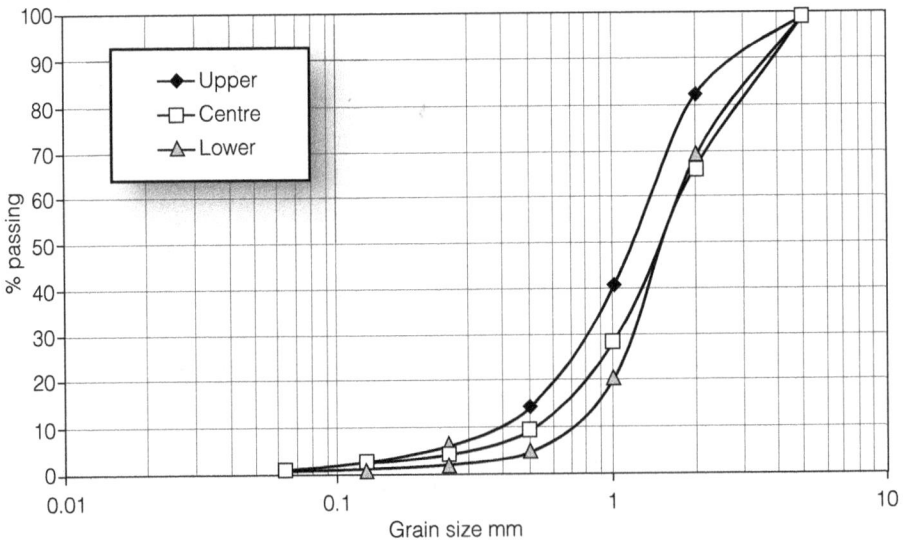

Figure 3.3. Manzamnyama River, Huwana – Sediment Grading Curve

Photograph 3.7. Sediment grain size gauge

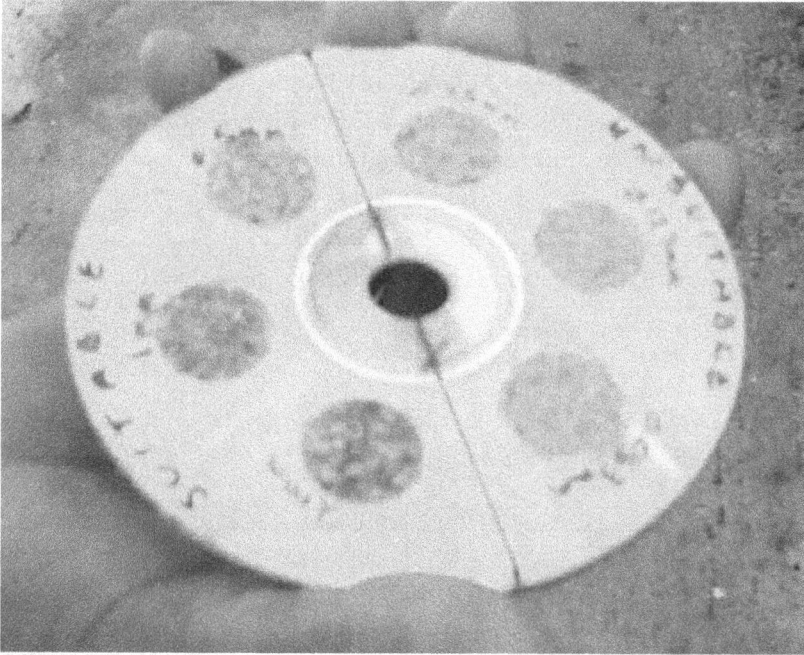

Visual assessments and simple equipment such as a kitchen sieve and a ±500gm tin and the sediment particle size comparator shown in Photograph 3.8 can be used to provide a rough and ready guide where purpose designed test equipment is not available. The comparator is made from two compact discs stuck together. The top disc has 20mm holes drilled through and the lower is a backing disc. The two together provide recesses into which particles of graded sediment have been glued and their size recorded for quick, visual comparisons with samples of river sediment.

Simple tests to provide an indication of porosity

Test 1: A rough and ready method of calculating porosity

1. Equipment — an empty ±500gm tin, sound and open at one end. An empty, clear plastic 2½ litre bottle with the top cut off to make a ±100mm aperture.

2. Method — fill the plastic bottle with 4 level tins of dry river sand, disturbed as little as possible but made level within the bottle.

3. Fill the tin full of water and slowly pour the water into the plastic bottle until the water-level is exactly at the surface of the sand.

4. If an entire tin of water has been added to the sand without overtopping the sediment level the porosity will be 25%. (One tin of water has been absorbed by 4 tins of sediment). Estimations of the quantity of water i.e. the amounts of a tin that have been absorbed by 4 tins of sand, will provide appropriate estimations of the porosity as shown in Table 3.3.

Table 3.3. Simple test to determine the porosity of sediment

No. of tins of water absorbed by 4 tins of sediment	Approximate porosity (%)
1½	37
1¼	30
1	25
¾	19
½	13
¼	6

Coarse sediment with a porosity of 20-25% is ideal for sand-abstraction. A porosity of 10-20% is likely to be found in fine sediment and can be useable. Sediment with a porosity below 10% will require multiple or specialist abstraction equipment and may have a low total yield. Porosity greater than 25-30% can be expected in gravel beds; however these are often not deep.

Test 2:
A simple field test with a kitchen sieve as shown in Photograph 3.8 can be used to gauge the coarseness of sediment and thus provide an indication of the void space and the porosity.

Test 3:
Comparison with known foodstuffs to gauge coarseness of sediment.

Permeability test
The rate of flow through sediment
A scientific experiment can be conducted with a permeameter to determine permeability. The test will indicate how quickly water moves through the sediment. However permeameters are expensive and not easy to use.

A kitchen sieve provides a handy field test for those who do not have access to specialist equipment. Typically more than 50% of the sediment will pass through a kitchen sieve with a 1.25mm aperture.

Procedure
1. Take an empty ±500gm tin and fill with a random sample of dry river sediment.
2. Pour the sample from the tin through the sieve. Tap the sieve several times to ensure all the sand that can pass through will do so.
3. Tip the grains that remain in the sieve back into the tin.
4. The material now in the tin that did not pass through the sieve should ideally be at least one-quarter of the volume of the tin (±25% of the total sample).

Analysis
A sample of sediment with approximately one third of the grains of 1.25mm diameter or larger will indicate a suitable site for a sand-abstraction installation. The sediment will be sufficiently coarse to create a void space with a useable specific yield.

If a kitchen sieve is not available, a less sophisticated method to establish the suitability of a sediment sample for sand-abstraction is to compare a sample of sand grains to well known granular foods.

1. At the proposed site take a handful of dry sand.
2. Trickle the sand from one hand to the other hand which is held approximately 250-300mm lower.
3. Repeat 5 to 10 times noting the size and distribution of the sediment grains as they fall into the lower hand
4. The observed sediment grains can then be compared with short grain rice, coarse sugar, salt and flour.

Rice size grains represent maximum water storage potential.

Coarse sugar represents good storage.

Salt represents low storage.

Flour or **mealie meal** represents poor water storage potential with poor potential for abstraction.

A good water storage site is therefore one with good porosity (large pore spaces for retention of water) and good permeability (to allow the passage of water through the sediment to the well-point). Almost invariably the two go together.

Photograph 3.8. Simple grading test using household sieve

Quick field test to determine permeability

A rule of thumb test based on the test for porosity can be used to establish a rough estimate of permeability.

The more fines that blow from your hand or from the kitchen sieve, the lower the permeability, with reduced water potential for abstraction.

Estimates of the volume of water available
A rough formula to calculate how much water is available
in a sand river aquifer.

The average width *(by measurement)*
× average length *(by measurement)*
× the average depth *(by probe measurement)*
× void ratio *(by estimate from tests above)*
+ recharge *(by estimate)*.

Chapter summary

The identification of a sand river that is suitable for sand-abstraction use and the correct identification of a prime water abstraction site are most important. The physical characteristics of a river must be closely studied to ensure that the most suitable site is identified, a number of tests should be carried out to establish the nature of the river channel and the volume and type of sediment. A grading analysis is required from which the porosity and permeability of the river sediment can be established and from this an approximation can be made of the water reserve and the overall potential of the site for the development of a successful abstraction scheme. With this information and the study of the river channel, a suitable method of water abstraction can be determined.

With an appreciation of the characteristics of a sand river and with a possible site in mind the next step is to review methods of water abstraction, or if an adequate site cannot be found, possible ways to improve the site.

4

Abstraction methodology

Description of abstraction systems

With the introduction of modern sand-abstraction several systems have been developed that enable the withdrawal of water from saturated sediment. Each system requires equipment that can be installed into water-bearing layers and that will obstruct the entry of sediment. For a system to continue to be effective it must remain at all times in saturated sediment which allows adequate transmissivity.

Water has to be separated from sediment
so that it alone may be abstracted

Present-day sand-abstraction water supply systems range in size from small-scale hand-operated systems through to large schemes powered by diesel engines or electric motors. Smaller systems are typically used for domestic purposes or as water supplies for livestock. Larger systems invariably provide water for irrigation or for larger domestic use such as farms, hotels and safari camps and can include complete water supplies for small towns.

Principles of abstraction — separating water from sediment

The success of each abstraction system is dependent on the optimum separation of water from sediment through the creation of a graded barrier within the sediment at the point of water abstraction. This requires the formation of a natural filter to prevent the passage of fine sediment. An artificial screen is required in order to create such a filter.

As water is initially drawn through a well-point screen it will contain fine grains from the sediment body in the immediate zone around the screen. Depending on the dimensions of the screen aperture, fine grains of sediment easily pass through the apertures but larger grains lodge against each other and are not drawn through. Smaller grains then in turn wedge against larger grains until there is no further passage of even the finest grains of sediment. In this way a natural filter is created around a well-point or infiltration gallery. Figure 4.1 shows the formation of a natural filter that has been created by drawing fine sediment through an artificial screen.

The dimensions of an artificial screen aperture are usually determined by the size and proportion of sediment grains within a sample of the sediment at an abstraction site. In order that a screen does not impede the flow of water from the alluvium the open surface area should correspond directly to the porosity of the alluvium.

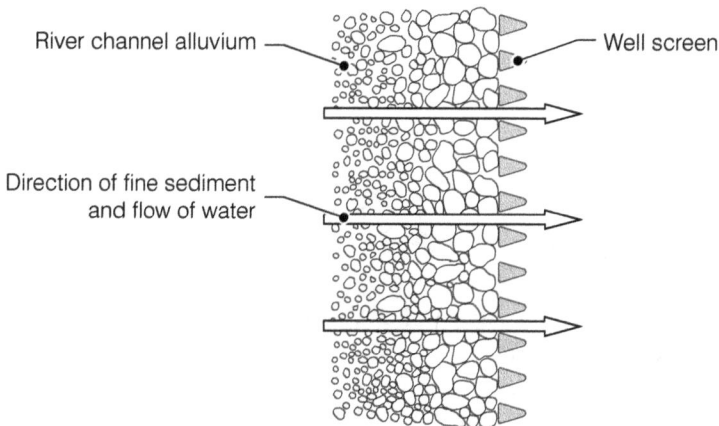

River channel alluvium

Well screen

Direction of fine sediment and flow of water

Figure 4.1.   Naturally developed sand filter

Ideally screen apertures should allow no more than 60% of sediment grades to pass through into the well-point. Borehole screen manufacturers typically state that the ideal screen should restrict the movement of 30 to 60% of all sediment grains. If greater than 70% of the sediment grade is drawn through the screen during the development of the natural filter slumping may occur around the borehole casing. However, this is not as critical in a sand river aquifer which is relatively shallow in depth and is not itself stable. This criteria may not always be possible, particularly where screens are home made, and in reality even a 10% restriction will generally be seen to work. If, however, the apertures are so large that a natural screen does not develop, the continual passage of sediment through the system will cause undue wear within the pump and abstraction system.

When the natural filter has been adequately developed, blockages at the screen face will be minimized and the void ratio in the immediate zone of abstraction will have been enlarged allowing a greater flow through the screen. Ideally the flow of water through the sediment will be laminar as shown in Figure 4.2 and will create no disturbance of particles that might cause a breakdown of the natural filter zone. In this way the sediment will remain undisturbed and the filter will continue to exclude the flow of fine sediment into the system, unlike turbulent flow that might dislodge particles that would allow further smaller particles to pass through the screen into the abstraction system.

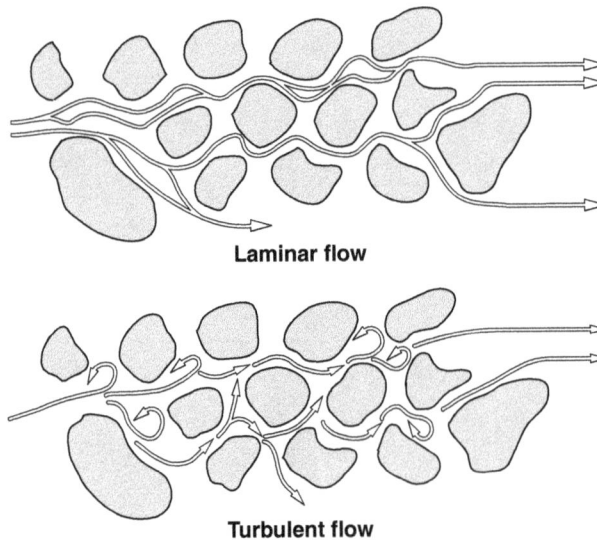

Laminar flow

Turbulent flow

Figure 4.2.   Flow of water between particles

A continuous slot screen is shown in Photograph 4.1 positioned within sediment that has been adequately developed as a natural filter. The principle of separation through the development of a natural filter applies whether the abstraction system uses a well-point, an infiltration gallery, a caisson or a well shaft.

The development of a natural, fine filter in sediment around a well-point screen also means that the water drawn from the sediment has been naturally filtered and is invariably safe water suitable for domestic use with few if any contaminants present. Typically there will be very little mineral salt contamination unless there is considerable abstraction from the river channel alluvium to the extent that there is excessive recharge

Where systems of separation are inadequate there will be excessive wear and breakdown of pumping equipment, pipe work will become clogged and the water unpalatable or unusable due to sediment in suspension in the water.

Photograph 4.1. An adequately developed natural filter

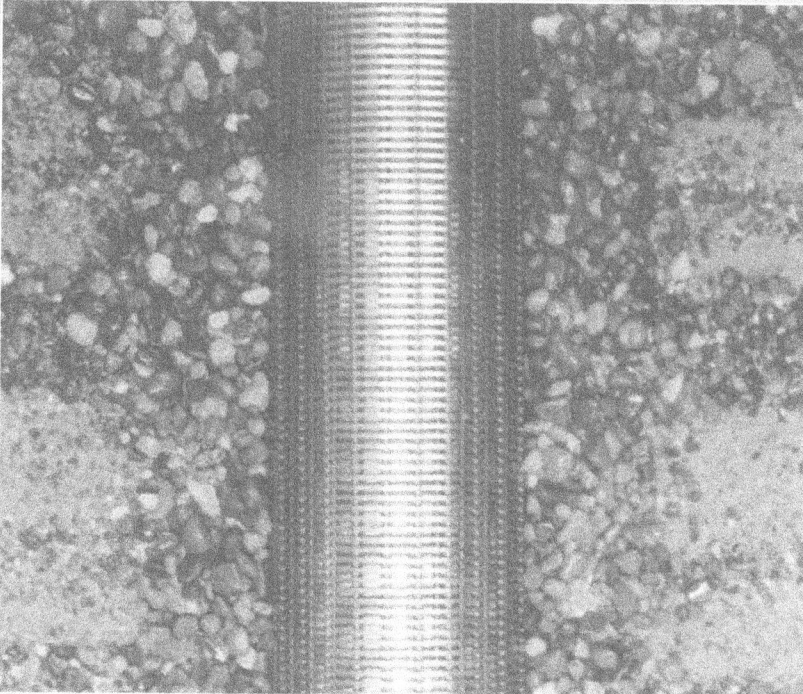

F. G. Driscoll

Well point Caisson/well shaft Collector well

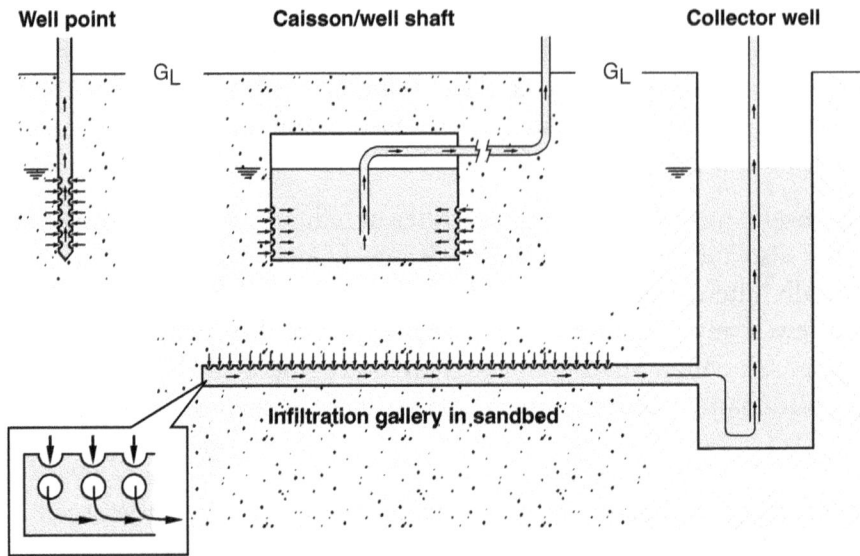

Figure 4.3. Types of abstraction equipment

and drawdown in the riverbank. If this occurs the mineral salts present in the soil are drawn into the alluvium from the riverbank and are then abstracted with the water.

Explanation of methods of abstraction

Methods of water/sediment separation

- Well-points (also known as well-screens or sand-spears)
- Infiltration galleries
- Caissons and sand wells

The basic systems of water/sediment separation equipment are shown in the schematic representation Figure 4.3. The illustration is not to scale.

Well-points

A well-point is a short cylindrical screen that is generally installed deep into the sediment in a river channel. Flow into a well-point is created by a pump which reduces the pressure within the pipe to less than that of the atmosphere, so that atmospheric pressure forces water into the well-point. Figure 4.4 represents a handpump well-point system to draw water from a sand river channel and pump it to a garden site above.

At installation a pump is used to develop the graded barrier around the screen and to draw water to the surface. A single well-point system can be directly coupled through a connecting pipe to a pump on the riverbank. Larger schemes comprise several well-points that join into a single manifold, (a larger diameter pipe), that is connected to one or more pumps on the riverbank.

Infiltration galleries

An infiltration gallery is a slotted or perforated pipe installed horizontally into the alluvium in a riverbed. Water flows from the sediment into the pipe through the pressure exerted by the hydraulic head of the aquifer. It then flows through the gallery pipe to a collector well in the riverbank. From the base of the well water can be drawn to the surface by a pump or possibly siphoned or gravitated to the surface at a lower point. The flow of water into the infiltration gallery develops a graded filter in the same manner as a well-point system but in this instance it is created by the natural pressure of the hydraulic head above the infiltration pipe.

The length of screen in an infiltration gallery will generally be of a greater length or diameter than a well-point as flow into the gallery is the result of the hydraulic head alone. In a typical riverbed aquifer the hydraulic pressure will be significantly lower than atmospheric pressure; consequently a greater surface area of screen is required to abstract water through an

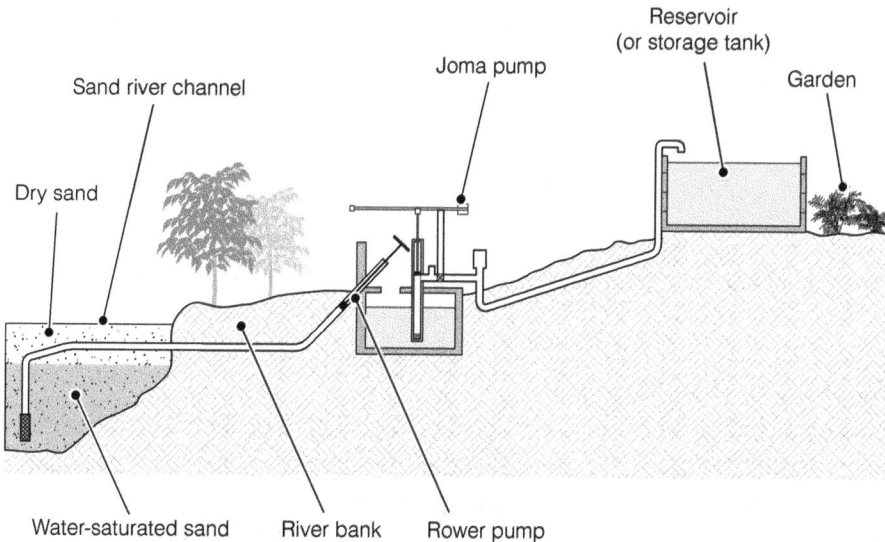

Figure 4.4. Layout of a simple well-point sand-abstraction system

infiltration gallery system than from a well-point. Thus in order to achieve the same yield, infiltration galleries will be either significantly longer or greater in diameter than individual well-points.

Infiltration galleries are often installed in shallow or fine sediment beds where there is poor permeability so that the increased length is of considerable advantage. Figure 4.5 indicates the layout of a typical infiltration gallery.

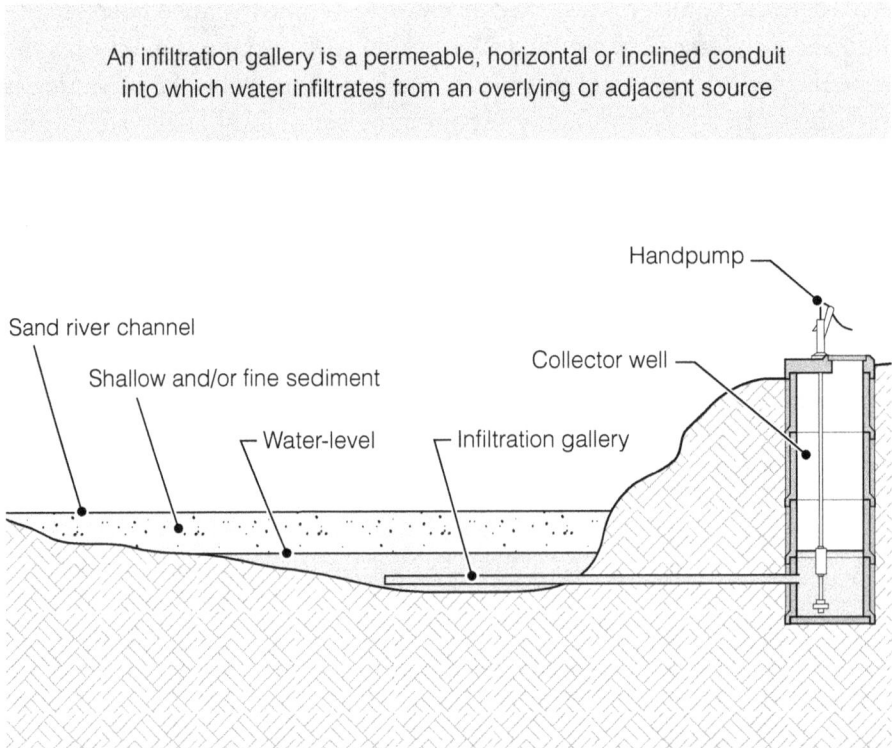

An infiltration gallery is a permeable, horizontal or inclined conduit into which water infiltrates from an overlying or adjacent source

Figure 4.5.   Cross-section of an infiltration gallery and collector well

Caissons and sand wells

Caissons and sand wells are typically larger structures than well-points or infiltration galleries and are installed directly into the riverbed or into alluvial riverbanks where there is high permeability. An offset sand well installation is installed in a riverbed and set into the riverbank as indicated in Figure 4.6. The lower sections of the wells are permeable so that water flows from the sediment into the well and eventually creates a graded filter around the base of the caisson or well shaft.

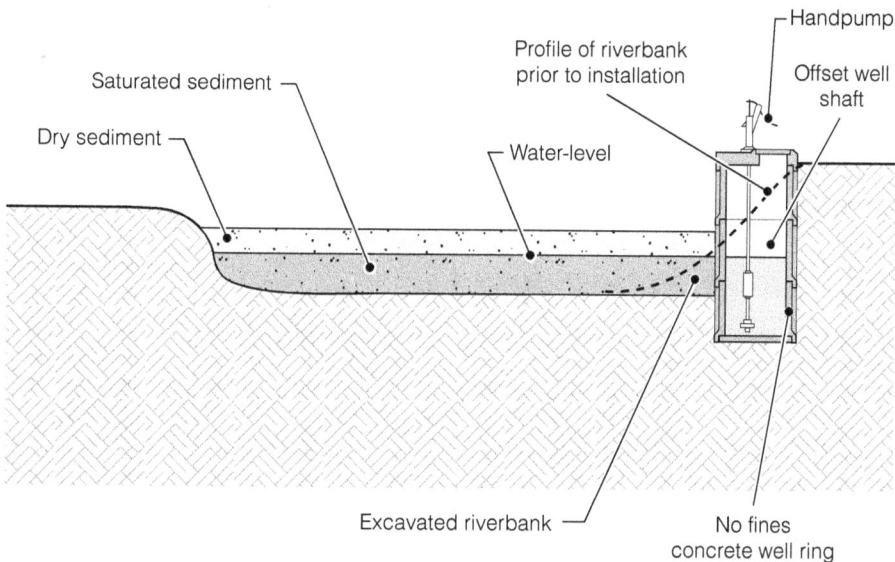

Figure 4.6.   Cross-section of an offset sand well

Methods of water abstraction

Once water is free of sediment a pump or water lifting device is required to raise it to the point of use. Small-scale well-point systems require suction pumps offset on the riverbank to draw off water. Both piston and centrifugal pumps are suitable and can be used on single and multiple well-point systems. Electric submersible pumps may be used in conjunction with larger diameter well-points where the pump can be installed direct into the well-point.

Where water is abstracted from a collector well that is offset on a riverbank any type of piston, centrifugal or submersible pump may be used. However, where a caisson or well is sited within a river channel and is subject to flooding, a basic abstraction system, such as a rope and bucket will be a better option. A submersible pump is a possible option in a sand well, provided the power cable and the delivery pipe can be installed below the level of sediment that will be transported to avoid damage.

> A sand-abstraction system is as reliable as its weakest component.
> Provided the screening remains undisturbed there is little to go wrong.
> To ensure sustainability the pump system should thus be as simple,
> basic and reliable as possible.

Handpumps provide a low-cost, sustainable solution for small-scale systems

Chapter 6 provides a detailed explanation of suitable pumps and pump applications.

Sand-abstraction systems

Equipment, use, situations and suitability

Screened well-point systems

Well-points are typically used where there is deep sediment within a river channel or alluvium. They are usually a cylindrical screen, some 32 to 200mm in diameter and are relatively short, generally only a half to 1.00m in length but may be up to 3.00 or 4.00m long where sediment is deep. Figure 4.7 shows a non-commercial round aperture, driven well-point.

Apertures are usually round perforations or slots, longitudinal or transverse to the tube. Slots may be straight or taper sided. A taper sided slot is radial and generally in a continuous spiral. It is wider on the inside of the screen than on the outside so that grains of sediment that enter the aperture do not become wedged within the slot as shown in Figure 4.8. Slots may also be embossed and louvered, open at the top, the bottom or both.

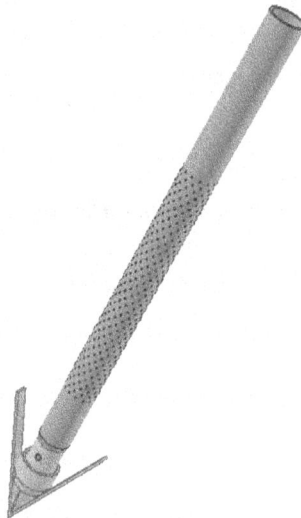

Figure 4.7.   Round aperture well-point

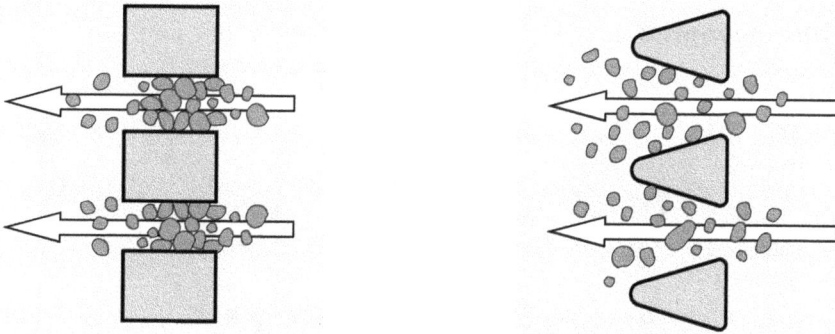

Figure 4.8. Parallel and taper slots

There are numerous designs of both well-points and screens and a variety of materials can be used in their construction. The screens may be made of uPVC, ABS or plastic, stainless steel, galvanized water pipe, copper pipe or wire-wrapped pipe and can also be made of concrete, fired clay, synthetic fibre or organic fibre. The apertures in the screen may be perforated, slotted or louvered; of detailed dimension and placement or random and tortuous. With slotted screens the slots may be short and transverse, long and longitudinal or a continuous spiral. In cross-section slots may be straight or taper-sided. Whatever the design each successful system is dependent on creating an extended filter within the sediment.

Well-points are generally installed vertically or obliquely into sediment and are inserted into the sediment either through driving or jetting, or simply through digging in. The installation should be as deep as possible in order to ensure that the well-point remains in water.

Well-points are easy to handle as they are small, short and lightweight. They are usually quick and easy to install and do not require complex pumping equipment. They are particularly effective in relatively deep beds of coarse river sediment in rivers of any width, although they are best suited where an abstraction site can be located within 30 metres of the riverbank.

Photograph 4.2 shows a sand river site best suited to a well-point and suction pump system. The river channel is wide, the gradient of the river low so there is a likelihood of an adequate depth of sediment and the riverbanks are low so that water can be delivered to the riverbank by a suction pump using atmospheric pressure.

Photograph 4.2. Chibabe River, Matabeleland South, Zimbabwe

Infiltration gallery system

One or more infiltration galleries are often installed together with a collector well where there is a reliable water supply, but where the sediment is shallow or fine and of poor permeability. The diameter of a gallery pipe generally varies from some 75mm to 300mm but may be as much as 500mm depending on the supply of available water. The length of an infiltration gallery may be as short as a few metres or as long as several hundred metres. An infiltration gallery induces the same mechanical separation of water from sediment as a well-point. Water enters the gallery from alluvium and is discharged from the gallery by the hydraulic head. However, there is generally only a small hydraulic head above an infiltration gallery and thus the screen section required will be of considerably greater length than a well-point screen.

In a small-scale scheme a single gallery pipe may be placed either across or along a river channel to discharge straight into a collector well on the riverbank. Where a single gallery is not practical, two or more pipes in a 'T' a 'V' a 'Y' or a triple forked (\I/) configuration can be installed in the river channel to increase the surface area for abstraction or as short lengths where the river is fast flowing. Large schemes invariably comprise a system of infiltration pipes placed in a herringbone or parallel grid system that discharges to a larger manifold that in turn delivers water to an abstraction point. Depending on their length a single or double gallery is generally sufficient with smaller schemes. Figure 4.9 indicates suitable gallery layouts related to channel width.

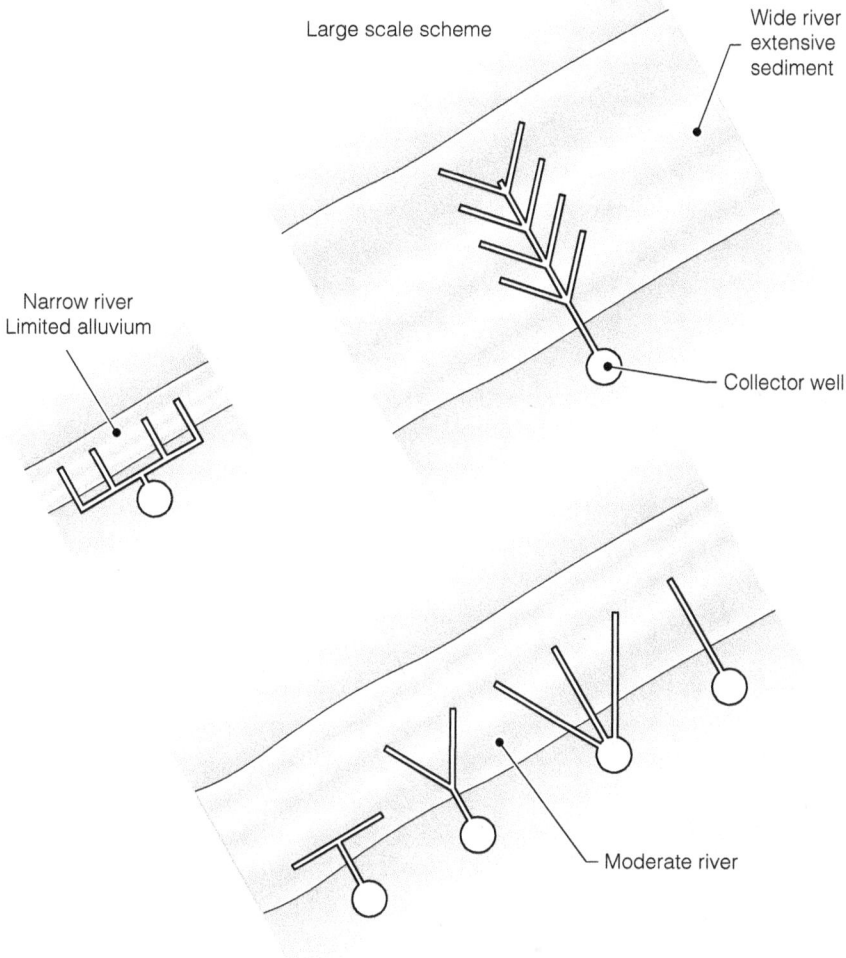

Figure 4.9. Infiltration gallery layouts

A successful installation necessitates much digging into both the river sediment and the riverbank to ensure that a satisfactory depth is reached that will keep the abstraction pipes in water bearing sediment. Unless earth-moving equipment is used, or shuttering has to be installed to shore the sides of the excavation, it is a relatively inexpensive system and does not require complex equipment or expertise to operate or maintain. Water abstraction systems may also be low-tech, requiring only a basic handpump or even just a simple windlass to draw water from the collector well. However, although a suitable technology in the right situation, it is difficult

Photographs 4.3 to 4.7
Infiltration well, Rundi River, Midlands, Zimbabwe

to ensure that any system of infiltration gallery is installed sufficiently deep in the sediment of seasonal rivers to be maintained in water at all times. In an ideal installation the infiltration pipe would be installed one metre deep in saturated sediment and if more than one, no closer than 3 metres apart and of a sufficient length not to create drawdown.

The collage of pictures (Photographs 4.3 to 4.7) shows a site where an infiltration gallery is best suited. The pump is installed high up on the riverbank where it cannot be damaged by flood water when the river is in spate. As the suction head precludes the use of an atmospheric suction pump a borehole pump has been used on the collector well. The pictures show the excavations and installation of a small-scale infiltration gallery, collector well and handpump scheme at Wasarawasara garden on the Rundi River, Zvishavane, Zimbabwe.

Infiltration systems do not necessarily need to be complex. In some situations rock-filled galleries have been used instead of infiltration pipes and as long as there is sufficient recharge through the soil to offset the pumping rate with existing head conditions, no gallery may be required at all. However, in any infiltration system the abstraction rate must not exceed the recharge rate and the flow to the wells must remain as close as possible to laminar so that sediment is not introduced into the well.

Infiltration gallery systems are particularly suited to installation in perennial riverbeds. They have been used with great success as small-scale water supplies at remote locations on the Scottish Isles through to water treatment and supply solutions for several cities in the North American mid-west, as well as a source of water to parts of New York City and Los Angeles.

Caisson system

Caissons and sand wells both use large diameter screen systems installed into sediment. The screens are typically from 500mm to 3m or even 6m in diameter and allow direct access to water. They can be installed straight into the sediment of a river channel or on a riverbank where there is alluvial soil with a high permeability. A caisson can be considered to be a well shaft that does not reach the surface. It is generally covered by a slab with a narrow diameter connection either vertically to the surface or horizontally to a sump on the riverbank.

Photograph 4.8 shows a sand river site that would be suited to water abstraction through a caisson or hydrodynamic well. The site comprises a

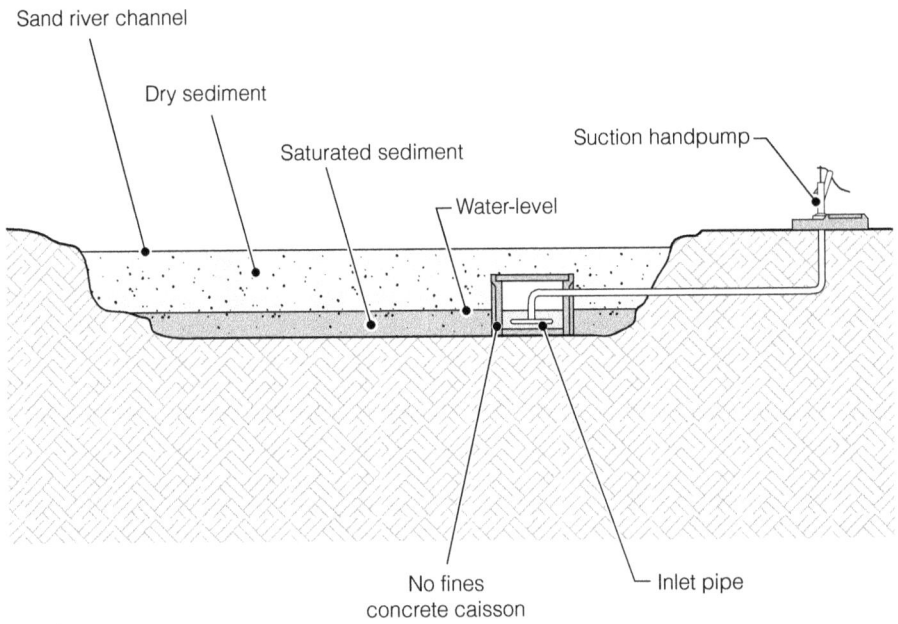

Sand river channel

Dry sediment

Saturated sediment

Suction handpump

Water-level

No fines
concrete caisson

Inlet pipe

Figure 4.10. Riverbed caisson

Photograph 4.8. Dongamuzi River, Matabeleland North, Zimbabwe

narrow stream with a low water retention potential where a large diameter shaft can be constructed deep in the centre of the channel to draw water from a large area.

In the lower sections caissons and wells are typically constructed of no-fines concrete or brickwork with no mortar between the vertical joints but also may be of steel or fibre-glass and slotted or drilled to create a screen. A caisson is typically cylindrical and depending on the nature of the screen and the diameter of the caisson, screen entrance velocities are likely to be particularly low, sufficient to maintain laminar flow to the screen. Such a large surface area within water bearing sediment and the subsequently low transmissivity rates make caissons particularly suitable for use in fine sediments.

Due to the mass of a caisson, it is necessary to install the structure on the floor of the riverbed for stability. The well-rings should not extend to the surface sediment but remain a half metre or so below the surface of the sediment to reduce the surface area when the river flows and when sediment and debris are transported through the channel. The well shaft is covered with a concrete slab and water is abstracted from the well by a suction pump which is sited in a sump on the riverbank or from a submersible pump installed within the caisson. Figure 4.10 shows a type of riverbed caisson that has been used on small rivers in Botswana by the Rural Industries Innovation Centre (RIIC), Kanye, Botswana.

The system is more awkward to install than a well-point system due to its bulk and the digging required to lower it onto the riverbed. Because of the large surface area from which abstraction takes place it may be possible to use a caisson where silt accumulates. However, although water can be drawn from very fine sediment, recharge will be slow, particularly where there are layers of silt to impede the flow of water to the abstraction zone of the caisson and thus abstraction may not ultimately be successful in silt conditions. Photograph 4.9 shows the installation of the solid upper sections of several concrete caissons which will be connected by a manifold.

Sand well system

The most basic method of drawing water from a sand river is from an open depression excavated in the river sediment, referred to as a sand well or scoop well. The natural upgrade of this traditional form of open well is a lined well. However, a dug well direct into river sediment is liable to be damaged by river flow, either demolished by the flow of water or in-filled by sediment.

Photograph 4.9. Installation of concrete caissons in the Rundi River, Zimbabwe

Sand wells are thus best installed into alluvial riverbanks close to the river channel where they can draw water from the river alluvium or dug into the side of the riverbank where they can interface directly with the sediment in the river channel as shown in Figure 4.11.

A sand well, as in Figure 4.12, that can be installed within a river channel and that allows floodwater to pass over without damage or any in-filling has been designed by Erik Nissen-Petersen, ASAL Consultants, Nairobi, Kenya. The well shaft is constructed from radiused concrete blocks with the lower eight courses laid without building mortar to allow infiltration into the well. The top of the well protrudes from the surface of the river sediment and is surrounded with rock and rubble overlaid with concrete. This headwork is of a hydrodynamic shape and has a cover to prevent river sediment filling the well shaft. The shape of the well head is akin to that of an up-turned boat, which allows water to flow around and over the structure and does not collect the debris carried by the river. This debris could build up around the well head and lead to its being washed away or to the destruction of the well shaft. Such a structure is probably best used within the sediment of river channels with low porosity and poor permeability. Here excavations can be made to the riverbed and the sediment has some stability, with little sediment transported through the river channel. In these conditions a degree of protection can be expected for a sand well shaft.

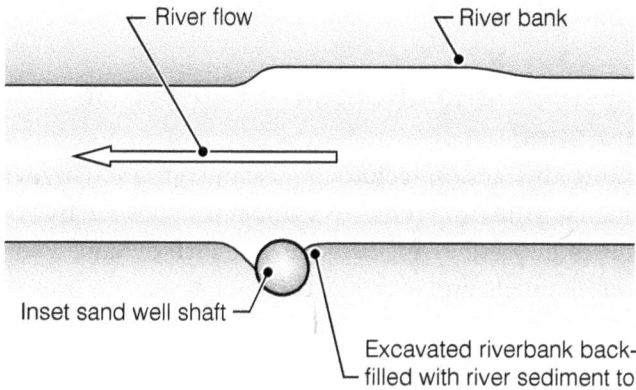

Figure 4.11. Riverbank site of an offset sand well

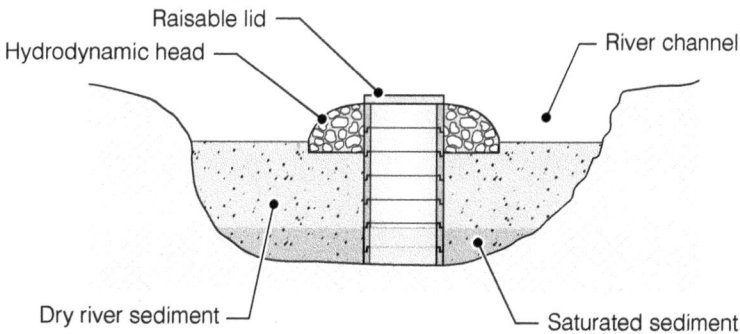

Figure 4.12. Hydrodynamic well head in a sand river channel

Each system, whether well-point, infiltration gallery, caisson or sand well requires installing into river sediment as deeply as possible. As the water-level drops during the dry season so it may be necessary to lower the screen or water separation area in order that water may continue to be abstracted satisfactorily. An installation is only complete once a level has been reached where the screen remains in water year round. This process may be achieved within a year or over several years with the final depth only being reached in a particularly dry year when the water-level in the river channel is at its lowest.

In adverse situations, especially in seasons of inadequate rainfall it is possible that alluvial river water sources become so depleted that abstraction systems run dry. An open system such as a sand well then has an advantage as there will generally be a small quantity of water, perhaps too small to be pumped, that will seep into the well and can be collected.

Related systems and alternative sources of water from sand

The use of sand-abstraction technology is appropriate wherever alluvium is unconsolidated. Alluvium refers to sediments deposited by flowing water and thus occurs in fossil riverbeds, the sub-surface sand and gravelbeds of paleo river channels and some of the flats alongside present-day river channels. The artificial formation of beds of alluvium in sand dams and hafirs (hafayer) create an additional clean water storage resource.

Sand dam

In situations where there is a limited accumulation of river sediment, water is only retained for short indeterminate periods during the rains. Although water losses from leaching, drainage and evaporation are lower

Photograph 4.10. Mkayi Wokhoza sand dam under construction

from sediment than from open water it is not always possible for water to be retained year round in all sediment beds. The construction of an open surface dam will increase the supply of available water but in dryland areas with high rates of environmental degradation and subsequent erosion there is often excessive siltation that may render a small dam useless in just a few seasons. However, where coarse sediment can be accumulated in a dam basin, water will be retained as if it were in river alluvium. Increasing the volume of sediment creates a larger water storage area. A sand dam, as shown under construction in Photograph 4.10, retains the sediment which is carried by the stream or river. The water is retained in the pore space in the sediment thus improving the supply of clean water and reducing the loss from evaporation.

In order to retain coarse sediment a sand dam is constructed in stages to a height generally not exceeding 1m in the first year and no more than 0.5m metres in each subsequent year. In this manner coarse sand is deposited behind the dam wall and the finer, lighter sand particles are transported over the wall. The construction process of a sand dam is shown in Figure 4.13. Through this construction technique the fine silt which would clog and limit the water storage capacity of the dam is not retained. The coarse material that is deposited constitutes a highly permeable medium with a large water storage potential.

As the spillway of a sand dam is constructed above the level of the river sediment, the masonry wall is built in steps in order to reduce the velocity and height from which the water falls thus preventing scour and undercutting of the wall that might lead to collapse. Water can be drawn from a sand dam through a sand well or below the weir through gravity by way of a pipe connected through the wall to an infiltration gallery laid at the bottom of the sediment. Vertical pipes can be connected to these to ensure that any silt layers which have formed do not seal the upper saturated layers from the abstraction pipes.

An advantage of a sand dam is that it acts as a large, natural, slow sand filtration system through an aerobic filtration process of sedimentation, straining, adsorption and chemical and bacteriological action. These processes are an effective method of removing impurities such as fine silt, organic matter, bacteria and most mineral salts.

Although not primarily intended to store water, erosion control methods may also yield useable quantities of water. Small dams, often called Check dams are small walls bonded into the base and sides of a gully to retain eroded topsoil in transport. Check dams can be constructed of locally available stone, either built with mortar or as a dry-stone wall. In effect they act as a micro sand dam by retaining water in the alluvium of the gully and also contribute to the recharge of groundwater. As check dams retain eroded material so they rehabilitate gullies and improve land that has deteriorated through erosion and where they retain sufficient water they may be used as a sand-abstraction water supply.

Sub-surface dam

A sub-surface dam increases the water storage potential of riverbeds where there is already a significant depth of sediment, but where due to excessive downstream drainage water is not retained year round. In areas

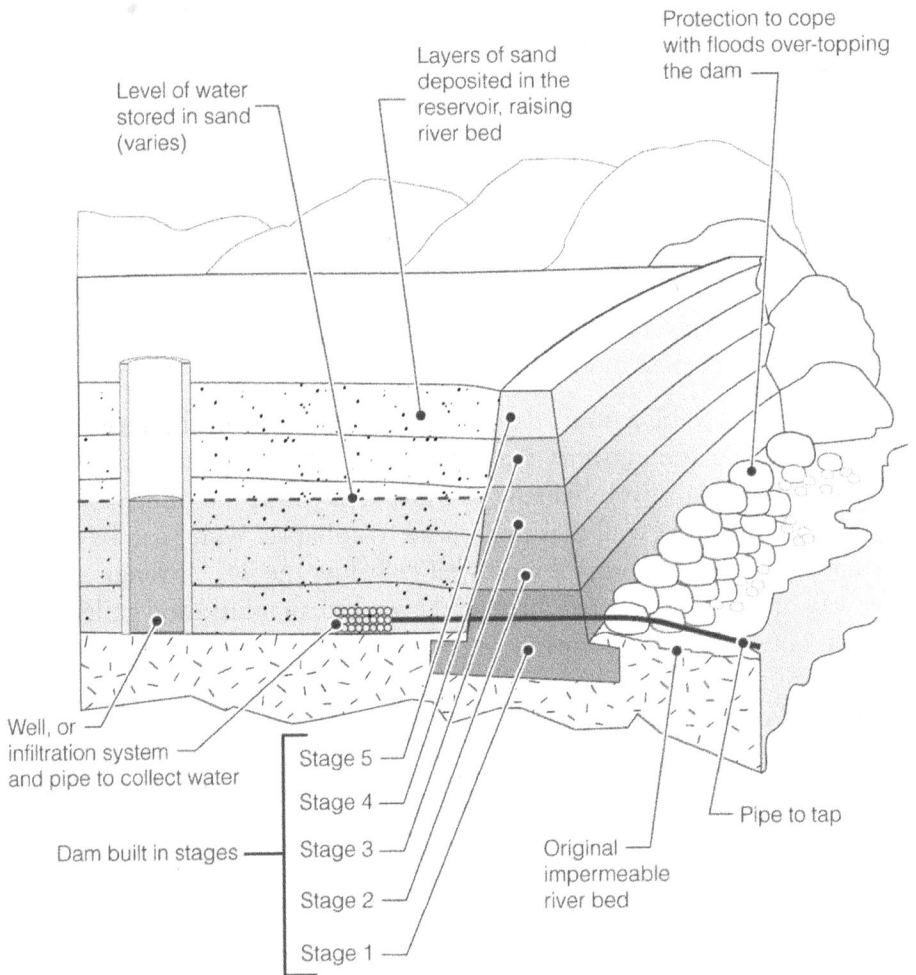

Figure 4.13. Construction process of a sand dam

where rivers have little slope many rivers have become so full of deposited sediment that the entire channel is clogged with alluvium. In particularly flat areas the river channels in some drainage systems are so clogged that when in flood the riverbanks are over-topped and extensive areas are liable to flood.

Where there is no appreciable basin the construction of a dam or a sand dam is not feasible, however the construction of an impermeable barrier within the sediment of a river channel will raise the water-level, reduce downstream drainage and entrap water which otherwise would be lost. Photograph 4.11 shows a sub-surface dam on the Swakop River, Swakopmund, Namibia that is constructed between a cliff on one side of the river and extensive wind blown sand dunes on the other.

A typical embankment dam or weir not only stores surface water in the open dam basin but through infiltration also in the sub-surface both below and upstream of the dam. A wall that is constructed on solid material in the base of a river channel and built to the same criteria as a regular dam will retain water in the sediment of the river channel and in the adjoining aquifer, thus reducing the loss of downstream drainage. In this manner there is an increase in the volume of stored water that can be abstracted.

As a sub-surface dam wall is supported by sediment on both the upstream and the downstream sides and as there is no increased velocity or vertical drop of water to absorb, where there is not excessive sediment transport

Photograph 4.11. Sub-surface dam Swakop River, Swakopmund, Namibia

through a river channel the construction of a sub-surface dam wall may be less substantial than that of a masonry, brick or concrete weir. However, as there is transport of sediment across the dam wall during river flow, depending on the volume of flow the top of a sub-surface dam wall should only be constructed to some 500mm below the sediment surface in order to minimize turbulence which in turn would reduce scour and loss of sediment that might lead to undercutting of the dam wall. The equipment and installation procedures used in sand-abstraction are equally applicable for the abstraction of water from a sand dam or a sub-surface dam.

In some river situations it is possible to construct a sub-surface dam using an impermeable membrane rather than a substantial dam wall. The process is both simpler and less costly to construct as it uses only polythene or butyl sheeting to create a barrier. A trench is excavated in the sediment of a seasonal river across the channel and to the base of the riverbed. The downstream side of this trench is lined with polythene sheet and the trench back-filled to leave a vertical, impervious membrane across the river to reduce losses of downstream sub-surface flow.

There are however, difficulties associated with the construction of a membrane dam:

- The river channel sediment must be fine and compacted as it is difficult to safely excavate a narrow trench in coarse unstable sediment, certainly to reach a depth where a satisfactory seal can be achieved between the riverbed and the membrane.
- The upper portion of a membrane may be damaged during periods of sediment transport through the river channel.
- A membrane is unlikely to be a permanent solution as it may well require replacing each year.

Wadi

Wadis differ from other ephemeral or seasonal rivers as they are essentially endogenous rivers in very arid or desert regions. A wadi carries the flash floods that occur following isolated but heavy sporadic rain, and generally has no defined source and no outlet although they may discharge into the desert. The volume and duration of flow in a wadi reacts directly to the intensity and duration of the storm creating the flow. Depending on the geology, the terrain and precipitation patterns, wadis range from short, sand-filled ravines to very shallow waterways, half a kilometre or more in width that are almost indistinguishable from the surrounding land as indicated in Photograph 4.12. Whichever waterway formation, when there has been sufficient precipitation to induce run-off, water collects in wadis and as the alluvium is unconsolidated, sand-abstraction technology can be used to draw water.

Sand wells have been successfully constructed in wadis in south-western Ethiopia and check dams constructed across wadis and gullies have been used to increase water supplies in several dryland areas.

Water losses in a wadi are typically high and in the Middle East attempts have been made to rapidly infiltrate water from a wadi into the sub-surface for groundwater storage. Further efforts have been made to link several small wadis through galleries or qanats to increase water reserves.

Photograph 4.12. Wadi, West Darfur, Sudan

B. R. Henson

Other systems of storing water in sand

Sand-filled water storage tanks — hafir

Pastoralists in the Ogaden and Horn-of-Africa traditionally store water in a hafir, an excavated, unlined pit that collects water from a nearby waterway or wadi. Hafirs are common sources of water storage in central Sudan where they range in size from 5,000 to 1,000,000m³. Because they harvest run-off water hafirs are prone to extensive siltation but when silted may not be rendered completely useless if it is coarse sediment that has been trapped.

The water storage period of hafirs can be increased by lining the pits with cement mortar or plastic, uPVC or butyl sheet. Smaller tanks have also been constructed that catch water from aprons or roof water collection systems. To reduce water loss by evaporation these tanks can be back-filled with sand and to increase their water storage capacity they may also contain porous hollow domed structures, sometimes referred to as 'beehives'. The design of a sand-filled hafir with beehive domes is shown in Figure 4.14.

Although tanks are generally open and used mainly for livestock watering or irrigation, sand-filled tanks have been used for domestic water. One

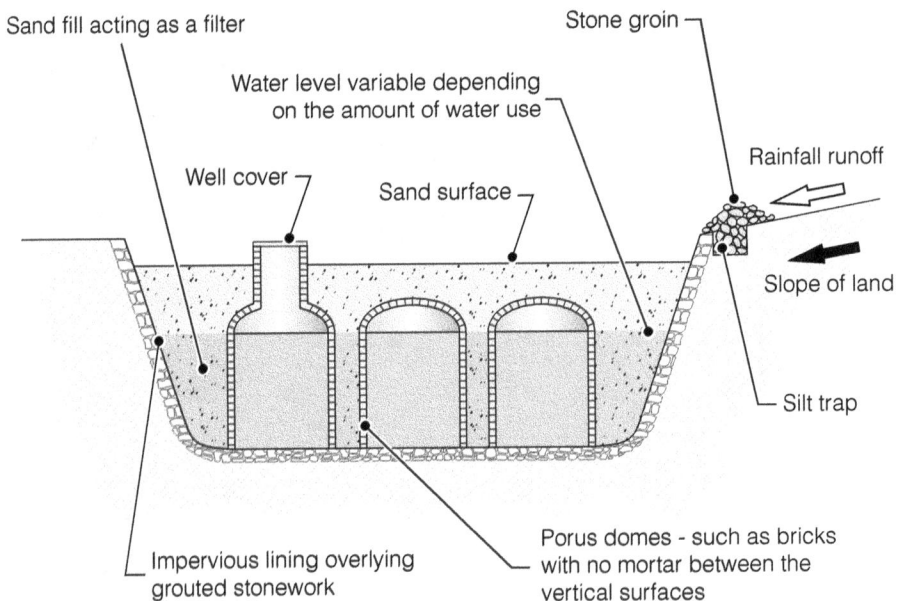

Sand fill acting as a filter

Stone groin

Water level variable depending on the amount of water use

Rainfall runoff

Well cover

Sand surface

Slope of land

Silt trap

Impervious lining overlying grouted stonework

Porus domes - such as bricks with no mortar between the vertical surfaces

Figure 4.14. Sand-filled hafir with water storage domes

Domestic hafir water harvesting system constructed in Serowe, Botswana for use by a family of five

The system comprised a sub-surface tank of approximately 76.5m³, rectangular in plan and trapezoidal in cross section with dimensions 6.0×9.5m at the surface and 4.8×7.3m at the base. The mean depth of the tank was 1.8m with a slight slope toward the water extraction end.

During construction 24 (6 rows of 4) cylindrical 'tanks' (nicknamed beehives) were erected inside the main tank and extended to 150mm below the top of the tank. Each beehive was made from concrete 'sausages' laid in a vertical spiral and dome-topped with an approximate volume of 1.75m³; total volume of beehives was thus 42m³. The 'sausages' were made from ±400mm lengths of 50mm diameter polythene tube filled with a weak sand/cement mix that was moistened and then held in place with short lengths of 4.00mm wire. These sausages were also used to protect the polythene sheet that was used to line the tank.

The interstitial space in the tank was filled with sand and with the exception of one access shaft the beehives were covered to a depth of 150mm. The domes and the upper sides of the beehives were covered with a sheet of clear 150µ polythene to ensure that water could only enter them after filtering through at least a metre of sand. Assuming an approximate percentage of voids in the backfilled sand of 25% the total water storage capacity of the tank was 50m³.

The sand surface in the hafir was covered with a sheet of 150µ clear polythene, with a further 75mm of sand on top of that for protection. The sheet was pierced all over with a garden fork to allow water to flow easily downwards through it, but restricted capillary rise to the surface to prevent excessive evaporation loss.

Clean water was drawn from the tank by a semi-rotary handpump that was mounted to one side of the hafir with a suction pipe inserted in the end beehive of one of the central rows which protruded above the surface to act as a well shaft.

system in Botswana provided household water from roof and yard runoff that was harvested each year in a sand-filled hafir. The water, which other than its passage through sand was untreated, was hand-pumped from the hafir to a roof tank and provided water for a family of 5 people for 5 years. To increase the water storage capacity of the hafir porous domes which restrained the sand were constructed in the base of the tank.

Sediment accumulation

Gabions, which are rock-filled wire frames or 'baskets', are used in erosion control situations to prevent the transport of sediment in flowing water. Where a series of gabions are placed across a waterway an increase may be achieved in the depth of sediment deposited within a riverbed. Although in such a system there is no seal or bonding of the gabion to the base of the waterway, the additional depth of sediment constitutes an increase in the volume of alluvium and thus the water storage capacity of the aquifer. The greater body of water is less subject to losses from evaporation and slower to drain downstream.

Sand and gravelbeds

Parallels can be drawn between the technology required to abstract water from sand rivers and the abstraction of water from sand and gravelbed aquifers. The materials and equipment required to draw water from river alluvium are similar to those used to abstract water from sand and gravelbeds. Although the installation technology may differ, a well-point screen is as appropriate in a sand-abstraction application as it is in a tube well or even a borehole. The criteria for screen technology, the slot aperture, shape and dimensions apply equally whether the screen is used in river alluvium, in a sand or gravelbed aquifer, a sand dam or sand-filled water storage tank.

The equipment and methodology required for the productive abstraction of water from sand-abstraction is also used in land drainage and the de-watering of construction sites. The design of materials and equipment required for the rapid absorption or infiltration of water from car parks or the continuous drainage of building foundations and basements, bridge pier foundations and applications such as the drainage of unstable motorway cuttings is also relevant to the technology of sand-abstraction.

Chapter summary

The essence of sand-abstraction is an adequate separation of water from sediment. This can be effectively achieved through the introduction of a screen into saturated sediment that will develop a surrounding graded filter to block the passage of sediment into an abstraction system.

There are a number of ways of preventing the movement of sediment and of creating a natural filter in sediment. A simple and effective method is to use one of a range of screens developed in the borehole industry, or to fabricate a screen using the principle of borehole screening. Screening can be used in relatively short lengths in a vertical position either as a single well-point or in multiple units with water abstracted through a direct coupled pump on the riverbank. Screening can also be used horizontally in longer lengths that discharge to a collector well set in the riverbank. A further possibility is the use of dug well technology to install caissons or sand wells into the riverbed or offset in the riverbank.

Inadequate sites can be developed through the construction of sub-surface dams that will retain additional water both in the river alluvium and in the adjoining aquifer. The construction of a sand dam or a series of gabions that will increase the volume of sediment in a river channel will automatically create additional water storage capacity. Sand-filled water harvesting tanks provide a further method of water storage that uses the benefits of clean water and reduces evaporation in the same manner as a natural sediment bed.

A decision is now required on which of the systems is the most suitable abstraction system for a particular site and the most suitable method of installing that system into a sediment bed.

5

Installation technology

Selection of an appropriate abstraction system

A water/sediment separation and water abstraction system must be suited to the hydrogeological conditions of the river channel and riverbank. The nature and depth of the river alluvium is a particular consideration. To aid the selection process, the appropriateness and advantages and disadvantages of each system are discussed here. For a complete description of various methods of sand-abstraction see Chapter 4.

Well-point and suction pump

This is a suitable abstraction technology for areas where the river alluvium is deep, relatively stable and is ideally predominantly comprised of coarse sediment grains. The main criterion is an adequate depth of sediment. Well-points typically offer an effective and versatile option for most sand-abstraction situations.

Advantages
- Low-cost — a straightforward level of technology with only a few basic materials required for fabrication and installation.

- Low maintenance system – materials required for maintenance and repair are usually readily available, no expensive parts or specialist repair tools or equipment is required.

- Satisfactory depth of installation easily achievable – system uses simple installation techniques to ensure a year round supply of water in the right conditions.

- Can be used in all seasons – whether or not the river is in flood.

- Multiple well-points can be joined for high volume schemes and/or where permeability is low where the alluvium is fine grained.

- Safe – no unstable well sides liable to collapse on users, unlike traditional open wells.

- Easy on the environment – installation is sub-surface and system requires little infrastructure and no brushwood fences to protect it.

- The system typically yields safe water suitable for household use.

Disadvantages

- Requires fabrication or purchase of abstraction or fabrication equipment.

- Requires a sealed system between the well-point and the pump – air leaks in the connecting pipes or leaking pump seals render well-point systems inefficient or even inoperative.

- Equipment can be vulnerable to flood damage – although the security of systems can be improved by anchoring the well-points to stakes, steel pipes or fence posts driven into the riverbed.

- Water may contain significant traces of silt when river is in flood.

- During effluent river flow or where there are high rates of abstraction, water in the river alluvium may become contaminated by the intrusion of saline salts from the riverbank. Mineral salts will affect the palatability of water and will contribute to encrustation around the well-point slots.

- In some situations, more often in perennial rivers, biofouling may occur within a well-point.

Infiltration gallery and collector well *(sometimes known as a false well)*

The system draws water from a large area making it most suited for abstraction in river channels with shallow beds of alluvium, or where the alluvium is comprised of fine grained sediment.

The layout of an infiltration gallery can be adjusted to the nature of the river. A single large diameter gallery across the river may be quite sufficient in wide slow-moving rivers whereas a river which is fast flowing with a high rate of sediment transport or a site on the outside of a river bend will require a number of short galleries, that might require anchoring to the riverbed with steel stakes.

Advantages
- No fabrication or complex installation equipment is required. There are proficient well diggers in many rural communities.
- Year round use — whether or not the river is in flood.
- Very basic abstraction technology — water can be drawn from a collector well by a simple handpump or a by bucket on a rope.
- Provides clean water that may be easily drawn from a protected well.

Disadvantages
- Infiltration gallery screening requires purchase or fabrication.
- Difficult to install to a sufficient depth to ensure satisfactory year round water abstraction.
- Requires a significant amount of work — digging and lining a collector well on the riverbank and excavating a connecting trench for the galleries in the river alluvium.
- Equipment can be vulnerable to flood damage — although this can be improved by anchoring the infiltration pipes to stakes, steel pipes or fence posts driven into the riverbed.
- Difficult and costly to construct in riverbanks that are not alluvial where rock breaking techniques or compressors may be required.

Caisson
A useful option in shallow, fine sediment where a pit can be excavated to the riverbed and a stable foundation secured for the installation. Ideally used in fine, stable river alluvium on a clay base or on bedrock where there is little transport of sediment through the channel.

Advantages
- Simple to construct — uses basic well construction technology, a skill many people in rural areas are conversant with.
- Suited to conditions of fine alluvium — due to a large screen area available for infiltration.
- Particularly suited to low-yielding small sand rivers where installation can be effected to a satisfactory depth — into or even through the riverbed.

Disadvantages

- May be difficult to install to a satisfactory depth, particularly in fluidized sediment.

- Installation requires a solid foundation.

- Where a caisson is submerged in sediment the top surface requires a cover to prevent infill and clogging with silt.

- As the screen is typically formed by no-fines concrete well-rings or courses of mortar free bricks, fine sediment is liable to penetrate a caisson that may then require de-silting.

Sand well

A larger structure than a caisson that extends from the base of the river channel to a height above the surface of the river sediment. Can be used as an offset sand well in an alluvial riverbank that has a high permeability and a good recharge to the well but may be used within river alluvium where suitable precautions are in place to prevent subsidence or in-filling with silt.

Advantages

- Simple to construct — uses shallow well construction technology, a skill with which many people in rural areas are conversant.

- Very basic abstraction technology — water can be drawn by a simple handpump or a bucket on a rope.

- A protected well can be used which will yield clean water.

- Suited to low-yielding small sand rivers where installation can be effected to a satisfactory depth — into or even through the riverbed.

Disadvantages

- Excavation in the riverbank or riverbed may be difficult to achieve to an adequate depth. Particularly in fluidized sediment, de-watering or well sinking techniques appropriate to unstable conditions may be required.

- Installation requires a solid foundation.

- Within river channel alluvium a well shaft can be vulnerable to physical flood damage and if not adequately sealed, to siltation.

- When installed within a river channel, system cannot be used when the river is in flood.

Figure 5.1 indicates the process of sand-abstraction site and equipment selection.

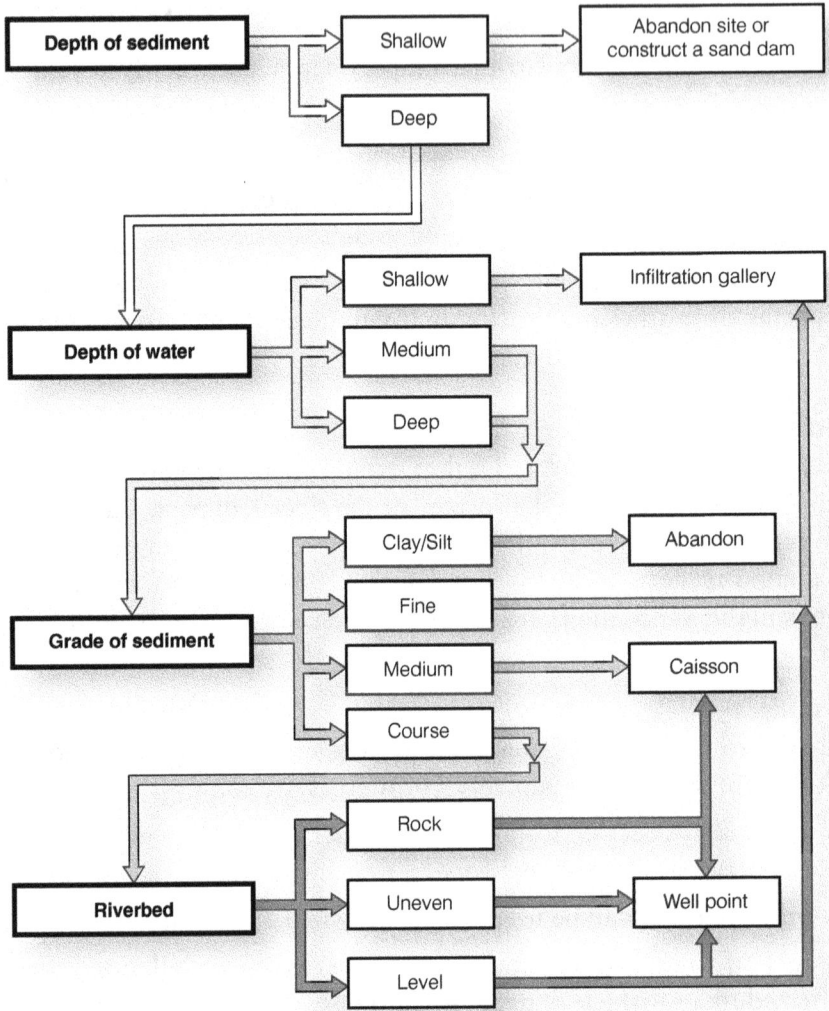

Figure 5.1.   Site and equipment selection chart

Installation selection procedure

The following is a step by step selection procedure that can be used to identify a suitable abstraction technology with the correct equipment design criteria and dimensions.

1. Select the abstraction technology

1.1. Appraise the site in the following way:

- Determine the depth of sediment.
- Analyse sediment particle size — assess from fine to coarse.

- Approximate the gradient of the river channel sediment surface.

- Determine the extent of the aquifer and calculate the volume.

- Observe the number of traditional open sand wells and seek the advice of local people with regard to permanence of water.

1.2. Determine the system best suited to the site conditions (refer to foregoing information).

2. **Select an appropriate screen** (refer to Chapter 3, sediment classification). This will invariably be determined by the abstraction technology 1.2 above, but the following should be borne in mind:

2.1. Optimum style

- An efficient screen will not become blocked with fine sediment grains – in effect the apertures should be self-cleaning, allowing every particle that enters the screen to pass through and not become wedged. A slot tapering in the opposite direction to water flow is generally better than a parallel sided slot (see Figure 4.8, Chapter 4). Unfortunately it is virtually impossible to construct taper-sided slots or holes in homemade screens with apertures of less than approximately 5mm. Probably the best that can be achieved in homemade screens is to ensure that apertures are as clean as possible with little or no swarf to block the movement of particles.

- In the construction of homemade screens longitudinal slots are difficult to fabricate in a pipe. Transverse slots are easier to cut but significantly weaken the pipe, which is likely to fracture between slot ends. Holes are easily drilled but particularly with smaller diameter holes it may be difficult to ensure a sufficiently large open surface area. Photograph 5.1 shows a range of well-points and screens. Photograph 5.2 shows a fracture that occurred in a homemade transverse slotted well-point screen.

- The screens of caissons and lined wells will typically be formed from no-fines concrete and will thus be random with no consistent aperture size and, depending on the materials and consistency of mixtures may include large orifices or conversely may not have a sufficiently large screen area. Photograph 5.3 shows no fines concrete well-rings of a type suitable for the construction of a collector well, caisson or sand well.

- The aperture dimensions of mortar free brickwork may not be sufficiently narrow to preclude fine sediment.

Photograph 5.1.   Selection of well-points

Commercial   Homemade

 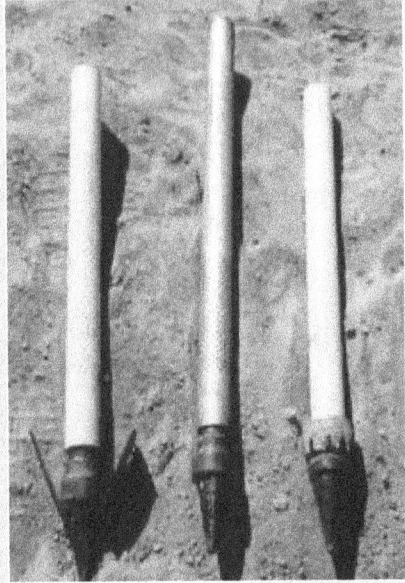

Photograph 5.2.   Well-point fracture between transverse slots

Photograph 5.3. No fines concrete well-screen

2.2. *Optimum aperture size*

- A standard recommendation based on traditional water supply borehole design principles is that a screen slot size should be large enough to allow 40 to 70% (nominally 60%) of sediment particles to pass through. In situations where the sediment is of a uniform grade (mostly single size particles) the lower percentage rates should be observed. Narrow slots tend to block more easily and satisfactory screens with small diameter holes are difficult to construct. In reality an acceptable screen can usually be developed even when a larger percentage of sediment grains pass through the apertures. Provided the sediment is not uniformly fine an effective screen will be formed but will take longer to develop as more fines will require extraction and consequently there may be greater wear to the pump. Ideally a natural filter should be developed in the sediment surrounding a well-point within 30 minutes of pumping. However, in exceptional cases, pumping in excess of this may be needed.

- Where sediment is homogenously fine a screen with small apertures must be fabricated. Depending on the sediment grading this can be undertaken with a 1.00, 0.75 or 0.5mm slotting saw or by drilling a pipe with 6mm holes and then wrapping the entire pipe in synthetic, non rotting geo-textile.

2.3. Optimum open surface area

- Depending on aperture size an efficient screen should ideally comprise 60% of pipe material and 40% of open surface area. However it is unlikely that a percentage higher than 25% open surface area will be achievable in a homemade screen and 10% could be the norm. Figure 5.2 shows a commercial continuous slot well-point screen.

3. Select suitable connecting piping

3.1. Class of pipe

- Piping is required with an adequate tensile strength, flexibility and a wall thickness that will not be damaged by the flow of river water and debris within the environment of river alluvium. Where suction pumps are used the pump and connecting pipes must adequately withstand the differential pressures that will be exerted.

3.2. Optimum velocity

- A well designed system has a screen with apertures that in conjunction with a further natural screen system developed within the alluvium will prevent the passage of all but the finest particles

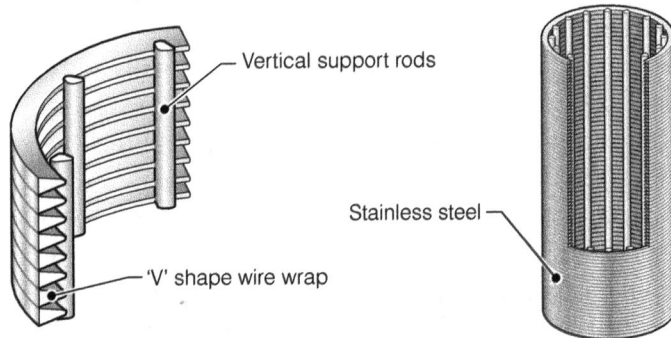

Figure 5.2. Continuous slot well-point

Although screen open surface areas are likely to vary from a low 1% in perforated pipe to more than 40% of continuous slot screens, the aperture size and open surface area of a screen is important. A high open surface area and a suitable aperture size and configuration is required to permit fine material to be removed quickly from the alluvium surrounding a screen in order that a zone of graded material can be effectively developed around a screen to increase permeability and recharge to the point of abstraction.

of sediment. In order to optimize such a filtration system and to prevent the further passage of sediment grains that do enter the system when it is developing or following disturbance of the alluvium during sediment transport, there is an optimum velocity of water flow in each section of the abstraction system.

Field experience indicates appropriate flow rates through a developed well-point screen system to be:

- At the point of abstraction 0.03 to 0.07m/sec — this is the velocity of the flow of water through the aperture area of a well-point. Entrance velocities into a well-point during the development stage of the natural filter when sediment particles are being displaced and repositioned are likely to be higher. Low entrance velocities are preferable, ideally slow enough to achieve laminar flow in the sediment. A low abstraction velocity also reduces the degree of incrustation that accumulates around screen apertures in groundwater that is high in mineral salts.

- Through a well-point and connecting pipe, 0.6 to 0.9m/sec — a relatively low velocity in this section prevents any further movement of particles that have been drawn into the pipework. In multiple well-point systems a large diameter manifold to reduce the velocity of flow to 0.3m/sec will further ensure this. The layout of a multiple well-point system showing a central manifold with multiple off shoots is shown in Photograph 5.4.

- Through the pump, 1.25 to 1.5m/sec — this is the generally recommended maximum delivery velocity of a well-point system.

The entrance velocity of water into an infiltration gallery and ideally a sand well-screen should be 0.006m/sec. This slow rate of flow ensures that in the creation of the filter in the sediment surrounding the gallery a minimum of fine sediment is drawn through the screen, which might create a blockage in the gallery pipe or in the well shaft.

An example of the calculations of the aperture size and pipe diameters required in the correct design of a well-point system is detailed in Appendix 1.

3.3 Drawdown

- By ensuring that as much as possible flow through sediment to a screen is laminar with abstraction rates not exceeding 1 to 1.5m³/hr per well-point drawdown in coarse saturated sediment in practical terms is not a significant factor. Due to the difficulty of installing infiltration galleries by hand to an adequate depth, drawdown is more significant with this system. Standard data collection procedures and formulae are available for calculating drawdown but again in practical terms, if the correct withdrawal velocities are observed problems seldom arise unless the water-level drops to the level of the upper apertures of the well-point or infiltration gallery.

Photograph 5.4. Installation of a multiple well-point system

In order to develop an efficient graded zone in the alluvium surrounding a screen, apertures that will permit the removal of 60 to 75% of sediment particles are required and in fine sediment up to 90%. The resulting natural screen should extend for as much as 300 to 600mm beyond the screen surface. The increased porosity and hydraulic conductivity of the graded material assist in the recharge at the point of abstraction, which reduces the drawdown and the possibility of an ingress of air during pumping.

Insufficient removal of fine sediment will prevent an adequate development of a natural screen in the alluvium.

Excessive removal of coarse sediment grains will lead to large amounts of sediment drawn into the delivery system.

Methods of installation

This section examines the methods of equipment installation, equipment and skills required, and the pros and cons of each system.

- Digging-in
- Driving
- Jetting

Digging-in

By excavating, either by hand or mechanically, each system can be physically dug into water yielding sediment.

- **Well-points:** a team equipped only with shovels is able to install a well-point into saturated sediment, however as with any digging, once fluidized sediment is reached it is difficult to dig any deeper and unless dug-in late in the dry season the water-level in the sediment is likely to drop so that the screen will be exposed before the river flows again. A slight advantage can be gained by forcing a shovel as deep as possible into fluidized sediment, then rocking the shovel backwards and forwards and working in the well-point behind the shovel blade.

  However, a largely untrained installation team with no sophisticated equipment can undertake digging-in. Photograph 5.5 shows a team of installation technicians digging-in a well-point.

Photograph 5.5. Digging in a well-point

E. M. Nyoni

- **Infiltration-galleries and collector wells:** as far as small-scale operators are concerned, digging-in is the most common solution to installing infiltration-galleries. In order to gain sufficient depth without the use of de-watering pumps, mechanical excavators or shuttering, the manual installation of infiltration-galleries can only be carried out at the end of a dry-season, before the onset of rains.

- **Caissons and sand wells:** Digging-in is the only way in which caissons and lined sand wells can be installed into river channel alluvium. When digging-in into unconsolidated alluvium it is a simple matter to place a well-ring at an appropriate point and to remove the material from inside the ring. By removing sediment evenly, starting in the centre and moving out until material is removed from under the well-ring the ring will be lowered evenly into the alluvium, securing the sides of the well as it drops. By placing a further ring on the top of the original ring the well lining is automatically placed and digging-in can continue safely in unstable material until water is reached. To assist the lowering of the lining the leading edge of the first ring can be bevelled to create a 'cutting' edge.

  Digging-in is also the only option for brick constructed caissons and sand well shafts located in a river channel. A frustum shaped excavation is required to a depth sufficient to ensure a satisfactory, stable foundation. The diameter of the base will need to be significantly wider than the outer diameter of the shaft and depending on the amount of fines and compaction of the sediment, the slope of the sides should be approximately 45° (the natural reclining angle of uncompacted sediment).

  Once again, as it is not possible to effectively excavate by hand into water saturated sand due to fluidized sediment welling up within the well lining or caisson, digging-in should be carried out late in the dry season to ensure that a firm base is obtained and to prevent the well running dry as the season progresses. As a caisson does not extend to the surface of the alluvium the sides of a caisson excavation must be cleared away, at least to the natural reclining angle of the material, as the digging progresses.

Driving and jacking

- **Well-points** — Where steel well-points are used these can be easily and quickly driven by a strong person with a steel sledge hammer.

Photograph 5.6. Driving in a well-point to 3 metres

They can be either vertical or inclined to the full depth of the riverbed sediment. Even where uPVC, ABS or plastic well-points are used, these can also be driven to satisfactory depths of 3.00 to 5.00 metres if equipped with a sacrificial steel point and a steel driving tube.

To achieve depths in excess of 2.00m a driving tube in lengths of approximately 1.50m is required; alternatively a temporary platform or stepladder will enable 3.00m lengths to be installed. To reduce damage to the steel by hammering, a length of timber is best held or fitted to the top of the pipe. However, even with a wooden block there is likely to be significant damage to the tube, particularly where there are threads. The driving tube is removed from the sediment when the well-point has reached a satisfactory depth, leaving the well-point in place. Photograph 5.6 shows a well-point being driven to a depth of 3.00m, with driving commencing from a step-ladder. Figure 5.3 indicates the protection that a block of wood can provide to a well-point driven with a steel hammer.

- Experience has shown that sediment can become compacted between the well-point tip and the driving tube making a fit so tight that when the driving tube is removed the well-point is also withdrawn! Two short wings attached to the well-point tip will

Reports from the mid-west of the USA indicate that well-points for tube-well water supplies can be driven into gravel beds to depths of 20 metres.

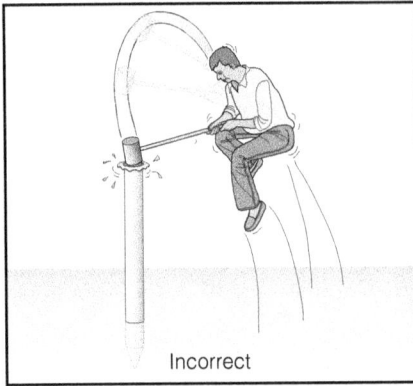

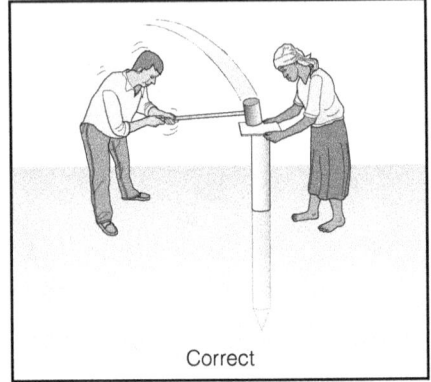

Incorrect

Correct

Figure 5.3. Driving in a well-point showing incorrect and correct methods

Photograph 5.7. Infiltration gallery and collector well on Blood River, South Africa

prevent this. A drawing of a uPVC well-point with sacrificial tip and anchoring wings is shown in Chapter 4, Figure 4.07.

- **Infiltration galleries** — Although beyond the scope of small-scale operators the British Geological Survey (BGS) has experimented with the horizontal jacking of infiltration pipes from collector wells below the bed of river channels. The system used was similar to the method above with a sacrificial tip and a jacking tube to push the tip horizontally through the formation. In order to undertake this it is necessary to construct a collector well of a diameter not less than the combined length of the jacking pipes and the hydraulic jack, (some 3.00m). Although there is a distinct advantage in placing infiltration pipes below the riverbed to increase the functional time of a well in seasons of low rainfall, the level of technology and the size of the well required constitute a considerable drawback. Photograph 5.7 shows the top of a collector well shaft, from which infiltration pipes radiate out under the riverbed.

Jetting

- **Well-points** — jetting requires an independent source of water. A motorized centrifugal pump is required to discharge water either directly through a self-jetting well-point or from an open-ended pipe attached to a regular well-point. Well-screens can then be pushed (jetted) through fluidized sediment into the lower levels of sediment whilst it is in an induced quicksand condition. The system operates more effectively in saturated sediment than in dry material where the water is likely to be dissipated laterally. Thus jetting is best carried out when the river sediment is fully saturated, or in situations where overlying dry sediment has been removed to expose water saturated sediment.

Figure 5.4 shows a self-jetting well-point and Photograph 5.8 the installation of a well-point by jetting. Finally Figure 5.5 indicates how the jetting process is effected as water is ejected from the open end of a pipe or a self-jetting well-point to flow back to the surface. It is important to maintain flow around the outside of the pipe or the water ejected will simply be forced into the underlying sediment and the jetting pipe will cease to move. A simple well-point can be attached to a jetting pipe with a piece of low strength string. When a satisfactory depth has been reached the jetting process is stopped and material will collapse around the jetting pipe and well-point. The jetting pipe can then be withdrawn by breaking the string leaving the well-point in place.

This system of installation is more technically complex and is dependent on a portable centrifugal pump, source of water, materials and equipment that are often not readily available in disadvantaged areas. By jetting when the alluvium is saturated to full depth there is an associated problem with not being able to sufficiently bury the well-point connecting pipe. In such a situation the pipe could be damaged during subsequent river flow.

- **Infiltration-galleries** — Some installation technicians report installing infiltration pipes by jetting. By moving a jetting pipe slowly sideways through sediment rather than downward, the surface becomes fluidized to enable an infiltration pipe to be inserted. The practice is not as straight forward as downward jetting and requires experience and a greater degree of skill.

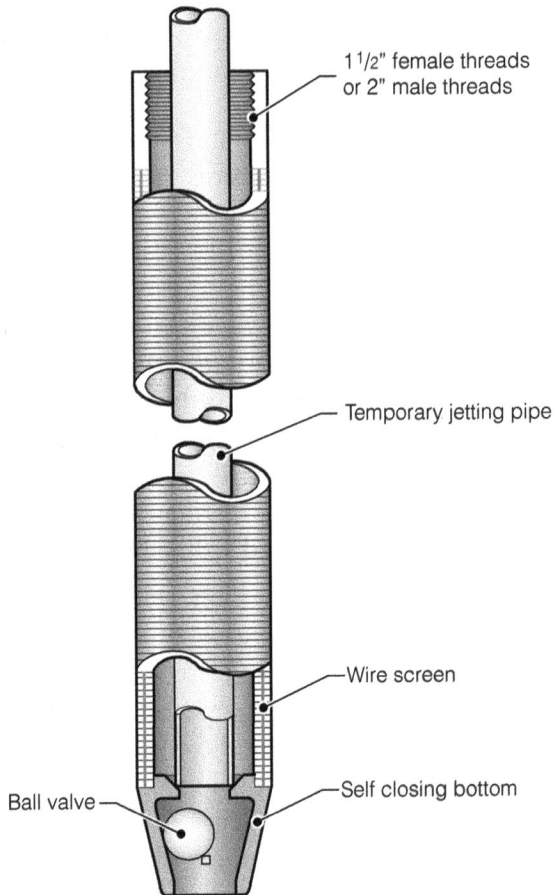

Figure 5.4. Self-jetting well-point

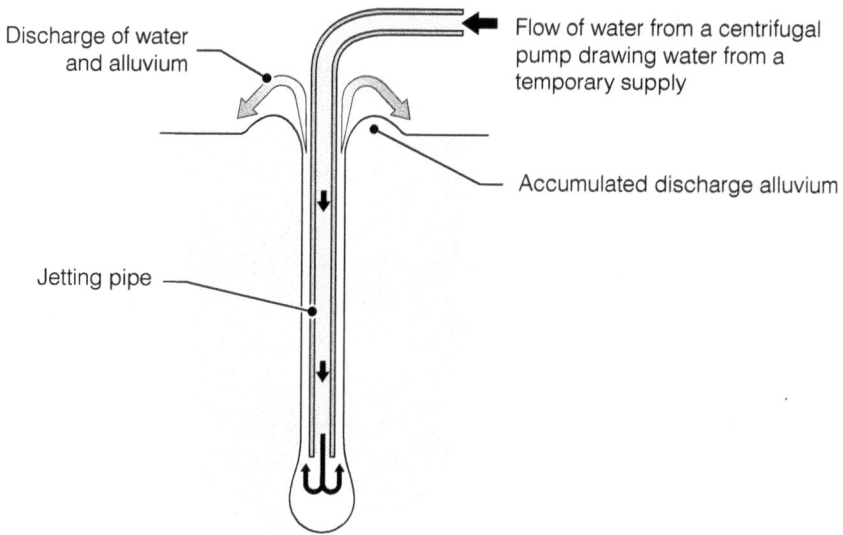

Discharge of water and alluvium

Flow of water from a centrifugal pump drawing water from a temporary supply

Accumulated discharge alluvium

Jetting pipe

Figure 5.5. The jetting process

Photograph 5.8. Installing a self-jetting well-point

Chapter summary

There is a range of screens and abstraction methods that are suitable for use in a number of differing situations. The correct system will depend on the nature of the river channel, the type and volume of the sediment, the site conditions and the requirements of the end users.

A well-point and suction pump scheme is a basic system that is easily installed and often provides a straightforward effective solution in conditions where there is deep coarse sediment. Either an infiltration gallery and collector well system or a sand well are appropriate where sediment is fine or shallow. Other abstraction systems such as caissons and sand wells are best used where there is fine sediment and particularly in smaller river channels where it is possible to excavate deep into the riverbed.

The installation of well-points can be easily achieved by either digging, driving or jetting them into deep sediment. The installation of horizontal infiltration-galleries is more difficult due to the difficulty of digging sufficiently deep in fluidized sediment. This difficulty may also occur when attempting to install collector wells, caissons or sand wells to an adequate depth.

In order to determine the most appropriate water abstraction system and installation method each system must be assessed against the river and sediment conditions, the materials available and the resources of the beneficiary community.

When the most suitable abstraction system has been decided an appropriate method of drawing water to the surface will be required. There are many methods of water lifting, of which not all are suitable for every system of sand-abstraction.

6

Pump technology

Methods of raising water

Once water has passed through a screen and is free of sediment it can be moved to a supply point. Whether or not water can be pumped immediately on separation will depend on the screen system and pumping method.

Well-point system

Unless the well-screen has a diameter large enough to install a submersible pump, water will need to be drawn into a pump through connecting pipes that in larger systems may include a manifold and a priming tank.

Infiltration gallery and collector well

Water must first gravitate or percolate into a collector well, into which a pump may be installed.

Caisson and sand well

Water will already be at the base of a large diameter shaft to which a pump or water lifting device can be fitted.

Once there is a source of water of sufficient volume, a pump or lifting device can be selected.

Factors to consider and to which a pump must be matched are:

- volume and surface area of the supply – the pump used on a relatively large body of water in a well may not be appropriate for the small body of water in a well-point

- rate of inflow

- depth of water, depth to water below the surface and the diameter of the screen system

- height to which the water must be delivered

- power options

- physical security of equipment

Pumps have many designs and incorporate one or more of several operating principles so that not all pumps can be used in all water lifting situations.

Pump and water lifting systems

The categories by which water-lifting equipment may be classified vary substantially both in terminology and type. Any one or a combination of the following general principles may be used to convey water:

- Gravity systems – water flows downward under the influence of gravity but cannot be raised to a point higher than the source. The system can only be used to transfer water to a lower point.

- Direct lift systems – a fixed quantity of water is physically raised in a single or a number of containers.

- Displacement pumps – water cannot be compressed (unlike air) and when moved through a pump it draws further water behind it. The volume of water that is pumped is equal to the displacement of the piston when it is moved. This is effected immediately in a direct lift pump where the piston is generally in water, but in a suction pump where the piston is above the level of water, air must be evacuated before the system is able to be effective.

- Velocity pumps – when water is propelled with sufficient momentum in the absence of air further water is drawn through the pump.

Table 6.1 classifies four water transfer systems that can help determine the appropriate pump in relation to an abstraction system.

The selection of a suitable pump for a given system will also depend on whether the pump is to be hand or mechanically activated and the identification of an appropriate power source.

Table 6.1. Water lifting systems and their suitability for sand-abstraction use

Operating system		System / pump examples	Sand-abstraction application
Gravity devices		• Qanat • Syphon	Very limited possibility in offset sand well or infiltration gallery and collector well
Direct lift Pumps – Shallow well pumps	Reciprocating	• Rope and bucket – free or windlass • Blair bucket pump • Shadoof	Sand well, Infiltration gallery and collector well
	Rotary	• Rope and washer pump • Persian wheels	
Displacement Pumps – Well and borehole pumps	Suction – utilising atmospheric pressure	• Rod and piston – above water-level – pump • Rower pump • Treadle pump • Diaphragm pump	Offset sand well Infiltration gallery and collector well
	Reciprocating Rod – deep well/ borehole	• Rod and piston - below water-level – pump • Afridev • India • Direct Action pump	
	Rotary	• Progressive Cavity pump	
Velocity Pumps	Rotary Pump – High speed mechanical, surface pump	• Centrifugal pump • Submersible pump	Well-point Offset sand well Infiltration gallery and collector well
	Venturi pump – Deep well/ borehole	• Jet pump	Offset sand well Infiltration gallery and collector well

The suitability of water lifting devices in sand-abstraction systems

Gravity systems

The most basic method of moving water is by gravity. However, as sand-abstraction screens are generally placed deep within river sediment it is rarely possible to use this method.

Suitability — used to great effect in traditional qanat systems that draw water from hillside aquifers. Can be used to siphon water directly from an infiltration gallery or from an offset sand well where there is a gradient with an appropriate delivery point sufficiently below and away from the river channel to which water can be gravitated.

Direct lift devices

Buckets, scoops and water wheels are used to physically raise a fixed quantity of water. Although many of these methods are simple and easy to maintain, with the exception of the rope and washer pump, they can generally only be used on shallow open wells.

- **Buckets** (with or without a windlass) and mohtes can be used in infiltration gallery and collector wells and sand wells. Although generally hand operated, these can be can be animal-powered (with the exception of a windlass).

  Suitability — Generally reliable and easy to operate and repair. However, they are often slow and inefficient and provide only a limited yield.

- **Shadoofs** can also be used on collector wells and offset sand wells. They are slow hand operated systems.

  Suitability — Easy to operate and maintain but have a low yield and a limited lift.

- **Continuous rope and washer pumps** (Figure 6.1) (also called chain and washer, Paternoster or Yeddle pumps). These raise water through a series of close fitting washers on a rope or chain that move upward through a pipe. Water is discharged as the washers leave the top of the pipe with the rope continuing to circulate and return the empty washers to the bottom of the well to draw in further water. Such pumps are capable of providing a useful output and can be considered an appropriate and efficient option suitable for installation on any lined well of a diameter and depth typical of a sand-abstraction system. Such devices are generally hand or animal-powered and are capable of drawing water from as much as 20 metres.

  Suitability — Well suited for use on infiltration gallery and collector wells and offset sand wells.

- **Persian wheels and scoop wheels** are generally capable of raising larger quantities of water than other direct lift systems, but have a limited lift height depending on the diameter of the wheel. A large diameter well is required for a large diameter wheel. Typically such water-lifting wheels are animal-powered.

  Suitability — Generally not suitable except on shallow, open wells that are not within a river channel and where a sufficient depth of water can be maintained to fill the lift buckets

Basic model pumps use
disks cut from rubber sheet
or the sidewall of a motorcar tyre.
More sophisticated models use
hydrodynamic plastic washers that
allow a film of water between the
washer and the riser pipe.

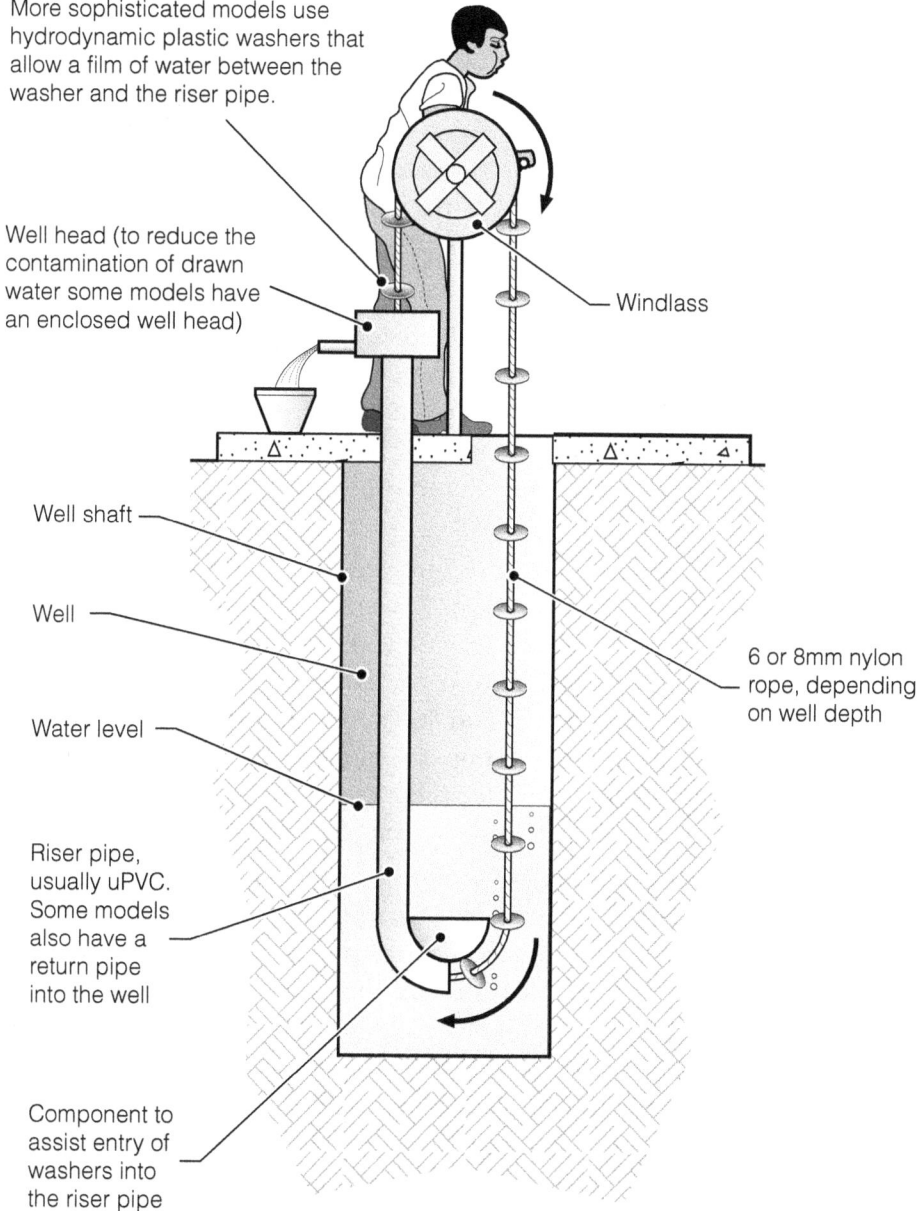

Well head (to reduce the
contamination of drawn
water some models have
an enclosed well head)

Windlass

Well shaft

Well

Water level

6 or 8mm nylon
rope, depending
on well depth

Riser pipe,
usually uPVC.
Some models
also have a
return pipe
into the well

Component to
assist entry of
washers into
the riser pipe

Figure 6.1.   Rope and washer pump

Displacement pumps

There are variations in the principle of operation within this category that use either a reciprocating rod with a piston and valves to lift water, or a rotating rod and rotor that moves water through a screwing process. Within the lift category there is a further variation where water is either raised through direct lift or through suction. Figure 6.2 shows the principle of (a) a direct lift displacement pump with the pump piston operating in the water and (b) a suction pump with the piston operating out of water creating a vacuum within the pump cylinder that is filled with water by atmospheric pressure.

- **Direct lift pump – piston pumps.** On the upstroke a rod raises a piston that draws water into a cylinder through an open valve. On this stroke water is also discharged from the pump head. On the downstroke the lower valve closes and water flows through valves in the piston to the upper part of the cylinder for the process to be repeated. Typically rod and piston pumps are hand powered but are easily mechanized with an appropriate pump head. Mechanical pumps operate at ±30 strokes a minute.

  Suitability — Pumps with a reciprocating rod that is located within a riser pipe and attaches to a piston inside a cylinder are generally used on deep wells and boreholes where the piston can be installed below the residual water-level. Many rural communities utilize such pumps and have experience, spare part and service/maintenance systems to ensure their on-going use. Pumps of this type may be used on collector wells and offset sand wells but as they are primarily for deep water applications they are generally cumbersome and over-designed for such relatively shallow use.

- **Direct lift, direct action pumps.** These pumps have a piston designed to operate within water and have an internal pipe that acts both as a piston and as a pump rod. As this is raised the piston valve closes so that the water inside it is raised and it also draws further water into the pump body. When the pump handle is pushed down, the internal pipe displaces the water that is in the pump body so that it flows into the pump 'rod' and in so doing water is also discharged from the pump. The pumps use basic principles of operation with a simple tee-bar handle to raise and lower the pump 'rod' and piston rather than a more complicated pump head with a pivot or pitman rod.

  Suitability — Generally more suitable than deep well pumps as they are better matched to the shallow depth and yield of a collector well or offset sand well and are more easily serviced and maintained.

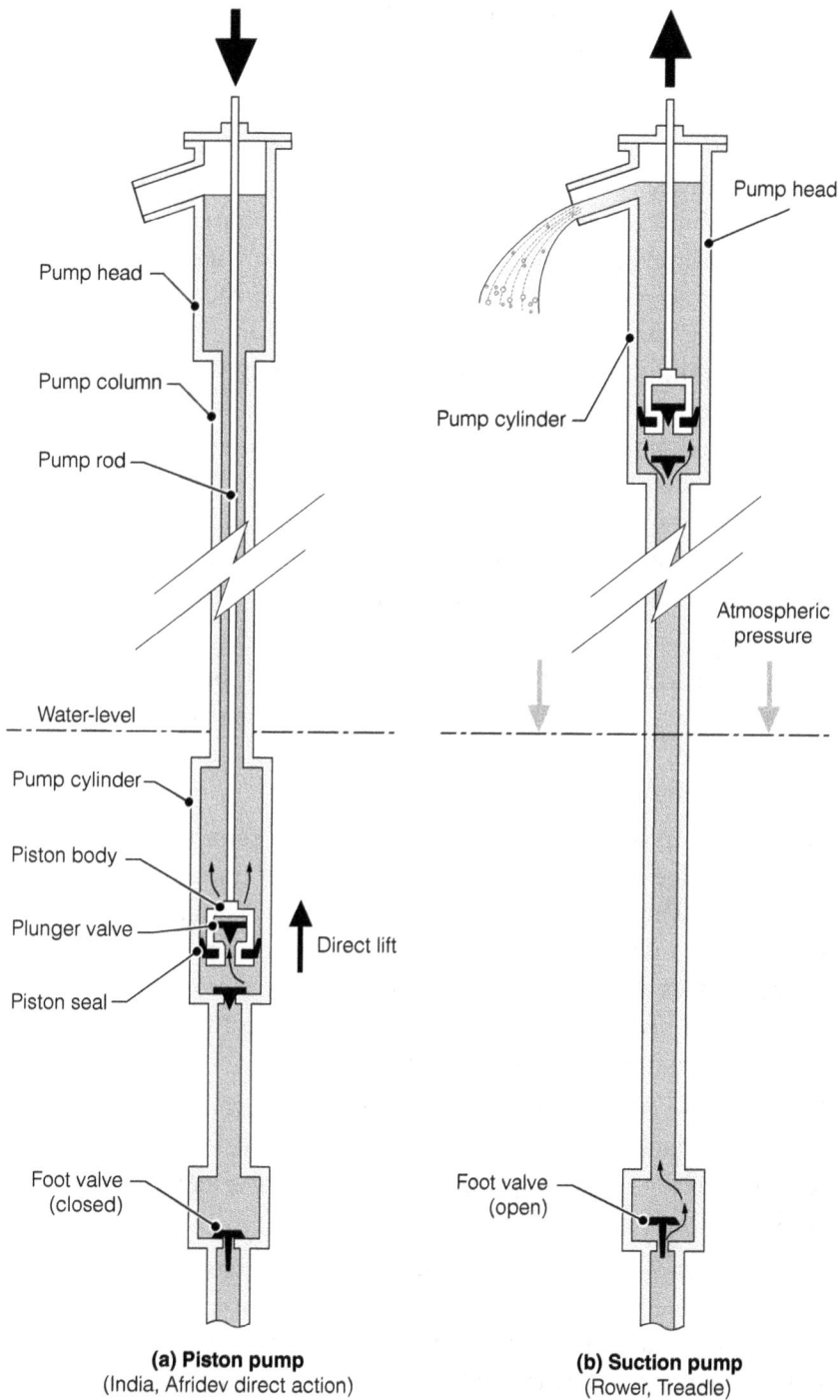

Figure 6.2.   Principle of two types of displacement pump

Figure 6.3 shows the components and working action of a commercially available Tara direct action handpump.

- **Suction pump.** Although now rather outdated terminology this pump is sometimes referred to as a bucket pump because of the cup or bucket seals that are used on the piston. The operating principle is as a direct lift pump but the piston is situated above the water-level. The pump has to be primed to displace air from the pump cylinder, pump column or connecting pipes so that water is forced into the pump cylinder by atmospheric pressure. The principle of the pump is then that of the direct lift pump. The efficiency of a suction pump is dependent on its capacity to evacuate air and on the altitude at which it is installed. As the head requirements of a sand-abstraction system are generally comfortably within these specifications these pumps are highly suitable for installation either on a well or coupled to a connecting pipe and a well-point, which obviates the need for a well. Such pumps are generally low volume hand (or at least human) powered pumps.

  Suitability — Suited to use on well-point, sand well and infiltration gallery and collector well systems. Also very suitable for connecting to well-points where the pump can be installed on the riverbank (within the limitations of atmospheric pressure and further limitations of altitude and pump efficiency).

- **Suction pump – lift or force pump.** A suction pump with two valves, one foot valve and one side valve where water does not pass through the piston. Water is drawn into a cylinder by a piston, through a lower valve as the piston is raised. However in this pump the piston is solid so water does not pass through it. As the piston descends it closes the lower valve and forces water out of the pump through a valve and delivery pipe in the side of the pump.

  Suitability — As the principle of this type of pump is similar to other suction displacement type pumps it is also suitable for direct connection to well-points as well as installation on infiltration gallery and collector well and offset sand well systems.

- **Suction pump – diaphragm pump.** A flexible diaphragm can provide an alternative to a reciprocating piston to move water. An upward movement of a diaphragm increases the volume of a pump chamber. In the absence of air, water will flow into the chamber through an open valve. A downward movement of the diaphragm will reduce the volume of the pump chamber and consequently the valve closes and water will be expelled through another valve and a discharge pipe.

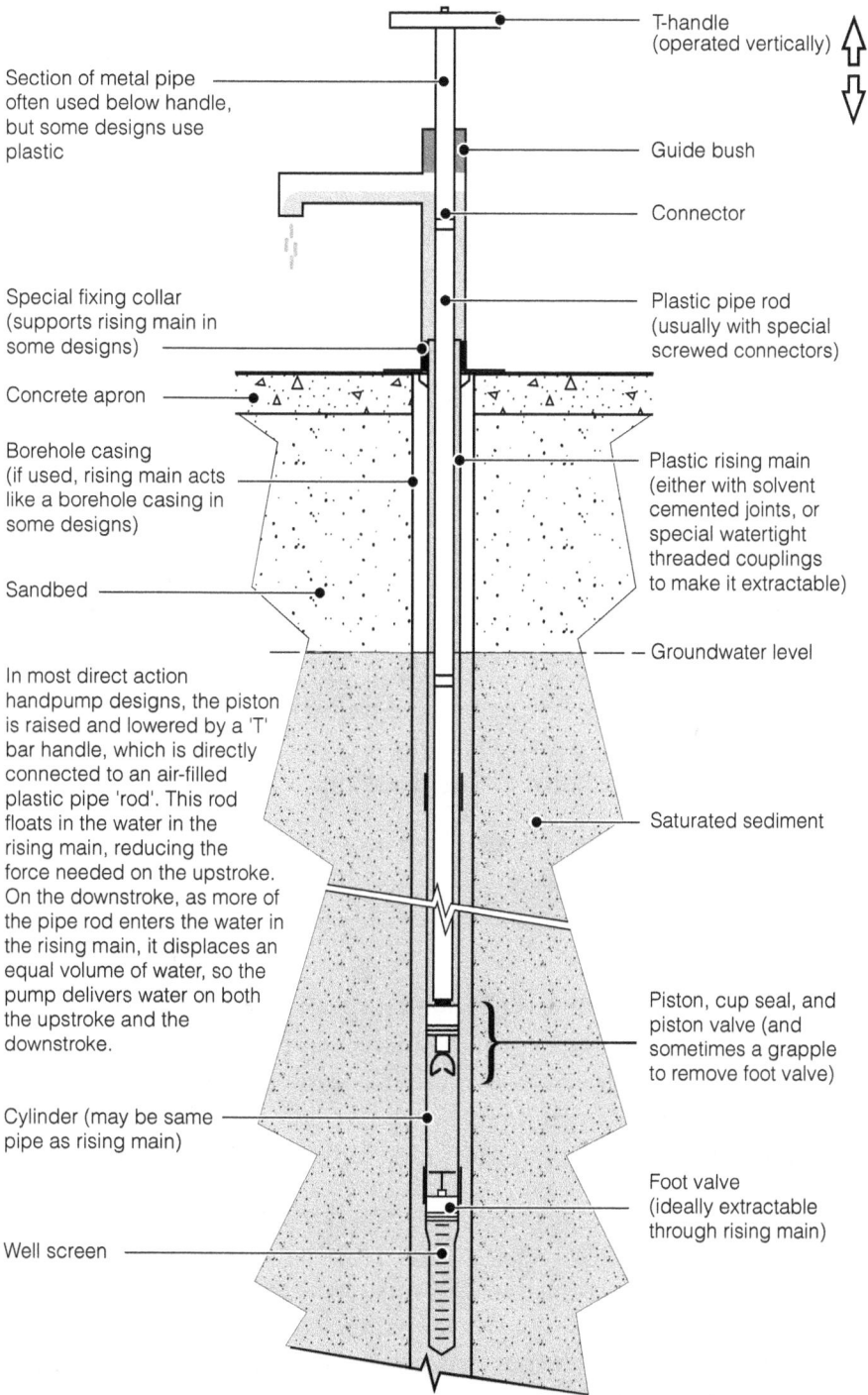

T-handle
(operated vertically)

Section of metal pipe
often used below handle,
but some designs use
plastic

Guide bush

Connector

Special fixing collar
(supports rising main in
some designs)

Plastic pipe rod
(usually with special
screwed connectors)

Concrete apron

Borehole casing
(if used, rising main acts
like a borehole casing in
some designs)

Plastic rising main
(either with solvent
cemented joints, or
special watertight
threaded couplings
to make it extractable)

Sandbed

Groundwater level

In most direct action
handpump designs, the piston
is raised and lowered by a 'T'
bar handle, which is directly
connected to an air-filled
plastic pipe 'rod'. This rod
floats in the water in the
rising main, reducing the
force needed on the upstroke.
On the downstroke, as more of
the pipe rod enters the water in
the rising main, it displaces an
equal volume of water, so the
pump delivers water on both
the upstroke and the
downstroke.

Saturated sediment

Piston, cup seal, and
piston valve (and
sometimes a grapple
to remove foot valve)

Cylinder (may be same
pipe as rising main)

Foot valve
(ideally extractable
through rising main)

Well screen

Figure 6.3.   Direct action handpump

Suitability — The principle of the operating system is akin to the piston suction pump system and thus diaphragm pumps may be used in the same situations.

Figure 6.4 shows the principle of diaphragm handpump.

- **Progressive cavity pumps** are sometimes referred to as helical pumps or by their trade names, Mono or Orbit pumps. Such pumps effectively move water in a screw process in a cavity created between a rotating spiral shaft and a specially shaped pump body. They produce a continuous flow, unlike (single action) reciprocating pumps that only deliver water on one stroke. Progressive cavity pumps comprise a single helix rotor within a double helix stator. A rotor is the general shape of a single twist and can be likened to the thread on a screw, while the stator is a double twist. When placed together a cavity is created between the rotor and the stator. When the rotor is turned the cavity effectively moves along the rotor maintaining a space between it and the stator. Water within this space is moved as the rotor turns, until it is discharged from the pump.

  Suitability — Suitable for use on sand wells and infiltration gallery and collector well systems as well as direct coupling to well-points where the pump can be installed on the riverbank.

Figure 6.5 shows the method used by a progressive cavity pump to move water.

Velocity pumps

- **Centrifugal rotodynamic (volute and turbine) pumps.** These use a single spinning impellor to draw water into the pump and to propel it rapidly. The high velocity that the water attains causes it to be discharged from the pump by centrifugal force. When this occurs in the absence of air further water is drawn into the pump body.

  Suitability — High speed mechanical centrifugal surface pumps are suitable for use on sand wells and infiltration gallery and collector well systems. Although a centrifugal pump of an appropriate size can be used on a single well-point, centrifugal pumps are particularly suitable for multiple well-point schemes that use a manifold and where the pump can be installed on the riverbank with a priming tank.

Figure 6.6 indicates the operation of volute and turbine centrifugal pumps.

Flexible diaphragm
in upward position

Pump operating handle

Flap outlet valve closed

Ball valve opens,
water flows into chamber

Upward movement

Flexible diaphragm in
downward position, forcing
water out of chamber

Flap outlet valve opens

Water discharge pipe

Ball valve closes, water
stops flowing into chamber

Downward movement

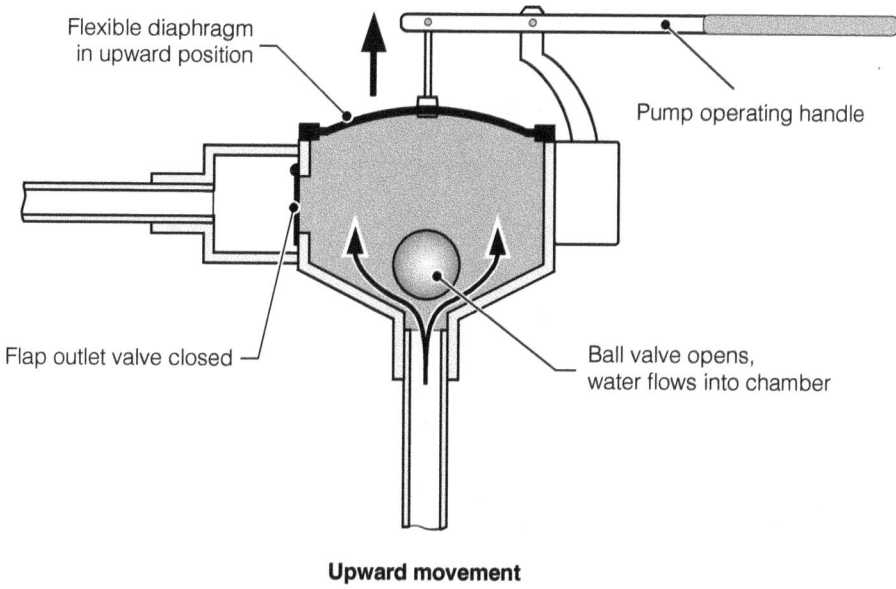

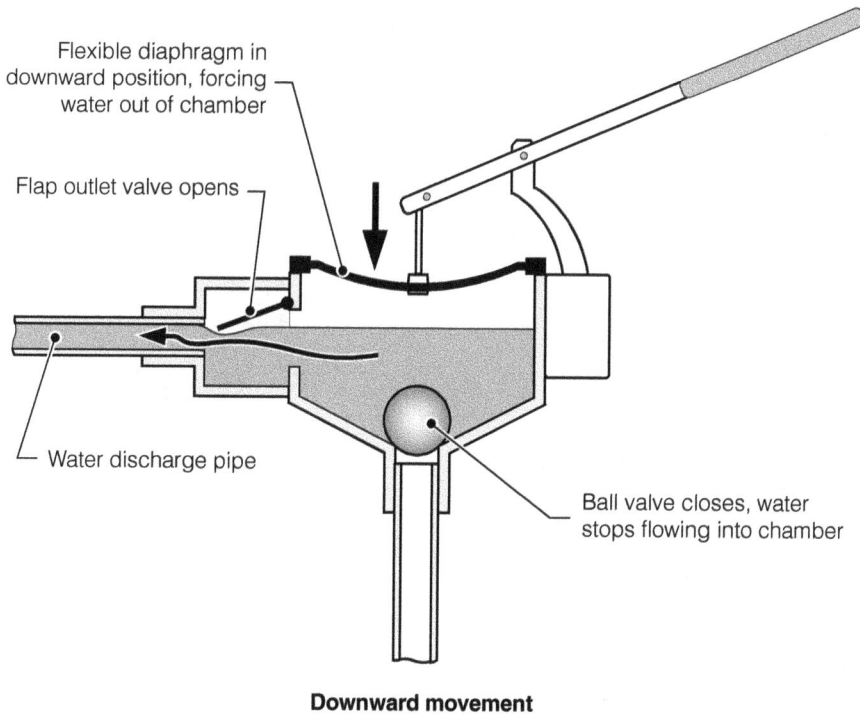

Figure 6.4.   Diaphragm pump

Rising pipe

Drive shaft

Stainless steel rotor

Rubber stator

Pump body

Inlet pipe

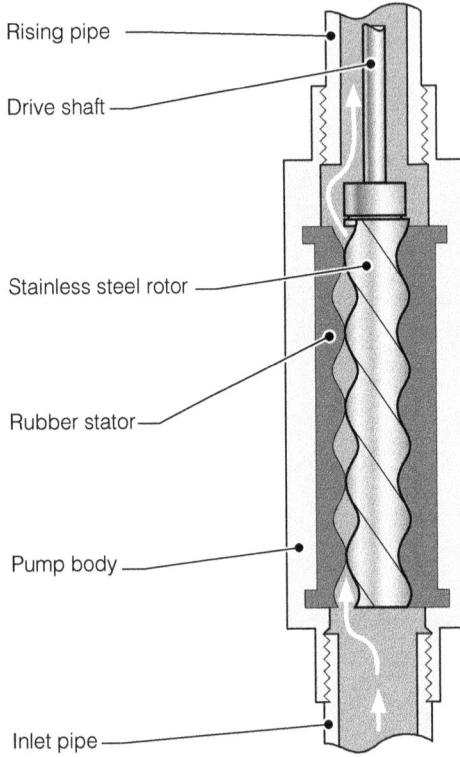

Figure 6.5. Progressive cavity pump

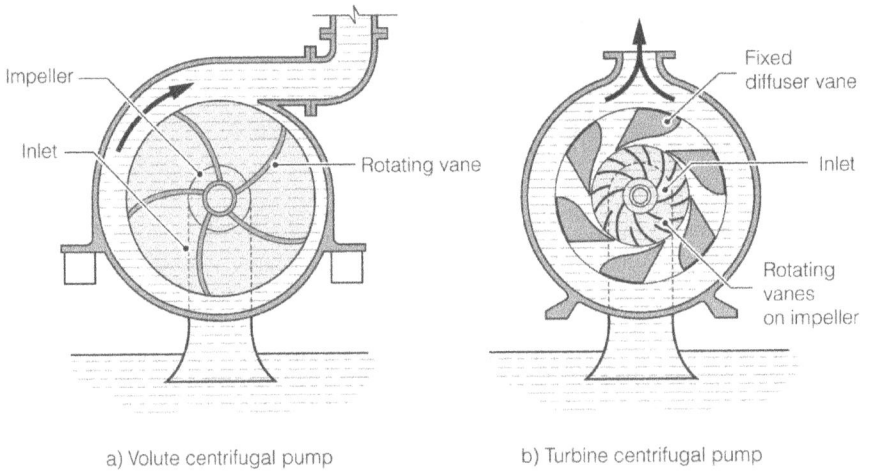

Impeller

Inlet

Rotating vane

Fixed
diffuser vane

Inlet

Rotating
vanes
on impeller

a) Volute centrifugal pump

b) Turbine centrifugal pump

Figure 6.6. Centrifugal pumps

- **Centrifugal multi-stage pumps** – these use the same principle as the volute and turbine centrifugal pumps but use a series of impellors to achieve the same effect. By coupling together a number of impellors directly to a sealed electric motor a smaller diameter pump can be achieved that can be installed as a submersible pump in deep wells and boreholes.

  Suitability — A suitable pump for larger schemes where it can be installed below the residual water-level. It is thus suitable for installation in caissons and sand wells and well-points with a diameter sufficiently large to allow the pump to fit inside. It is also suited to installation on infiltration gallery and collector well and offset sand well systems.

Venturi pumps

Use a high speed jet of water to draw additional water to the surface. To achieve this, water is pumped down a well or borehole in a pipe to a fitting that has a jet which discharges into a venturi. The temporary rapid increase in the velocity of water through the jet and venturi draws additional water into the flow, which together with the already circulating water is then delivered to the surface.

- **Jet pumps** use a centrifugal pump to create a flow of water that will draw water to the surface from depths of 10 to 20 metres.

  Suitability — Jet pumps have a limited application but could be installed on infiltration gallery and collector well and offset sand well systems.

Pump systems not appropriate for sand-abstraction use

The foregoing is a list of pump systems that might be used in sand-abstraction applications and is by no means a comprehensive list. Other pump systems are:

Ram pumps

As a ram pump requires a continuous flow of water to provide the energy to raise a smaller volume of water it is thus inappropriate as a sand-abstraction pump system in a virtually motionless body of water.

Deep water displacement pumps

Deep water borehole pumps are typically high specification pumps designed to raise small volumes of water from depths in excess of 100 metres and as such are over-designed for use in low lift applications.

Table 6.2. Suitability of typical pump systems for sand-abstraction use

Pump/Device	Advantage	Disadvantage
Gravity	• Basic • Low cost	• Generally unsuited to present-day applications
Direct lift – bucket and windlass	• Basic • Low initial cost • Low maintenance cost	• Limited yield. Suited only to sand well and infiltration gallery systems
Direct lift – rope and washer pump	• Basic • Low initial cost • Low maintenance cost	• Suited only to sand well and infiltration gallery systems
Displacement – suction - piston	• Versatile, general purpose pump • Ideal for small-scale schemes	• Best suited to small-scale applications
Displacement – direct lift, direct action	• Low initial cost • Low maintenance cost	• Suited only to wells
Displacement – diminishing cavity	• Efficient • Range of pumps available from handpumps to large-scale mechanized pumps • Best suited to large-scale mechanized schemes	• High initial cost • High maintenance cost • Intolerant of abrasive sediment
Displacement – suction - diaphragm	• Versatile, general purpose pump • Ideal for small-scale schemes	• High initial cost • Diaphragms liable to rupture
Velocity – centrifugal	• Efficient • Suited to large mechanized schemes	• High initial cost • Priming may be a problem • Not appropriate for small-scale schemes

Table 6.2 tabulates the advantages and disadvantages of typical and suitable pump systems.

Chapter summary

An overview of pumps and pump technology is provided as there is a vast array of pumps and pump operating systems that have been designed for particular applications. With the requirements of the various sand-abstraction systems it is apparent that not all pumps are suitable for use with all sand-abstraction systems. The suitability of a pump depends on a number of factors; the nature, size and location of the abstraction scheme, the volume of water to be pumped, the depths from, and the heights to which it has to be pumped; suitable power options and the resources of the end users. The physical dimension of apertures and access area of the chosen abstraction system will also affect the type of pump that can be used. A pump which is suitable for use with a well-point system will not necessarily be suitable on an open well shaft and a pump that can be used on a well shaft may not be suitable on a tube well shaft.

The selection of a suitable pump is crucial to the success and sustainability of a sand-abstraction system and requires careful planning.

7

Pump selection

Small-scale community-based systems

Rower pumps

The Rower pump is a simple handpump with applications not only suited to drawing water from most small-scale sand-abstraction well systems, but also directly from well-point systems. The pump comprises little more than a tee-bar handle with a short rod and piston and a non-return valve which all fit at the end of a delivery pipe. The pump is inclined at a 30° angle from the horizontal and as implied its name is derived from the 'rowing' action that is required to operate it.

In its basic form as a direct-lift bucket pump, water is discharged on the pull, or 'up' stroke as it flows from the open end of the pump cylinder. A Rower pump is thus unable to raise water beyond the height at which it is operated. However such a basic system does allow for quick and easy access to all wearing parts. In a less basic application the Rower pump can be converted in effect to a force pump that will deliver water to a head on the push or 'down' stroke.

The basic pump was developed by a member of the Mennonite community to draw water for small-scale irrigation project use in Bangladesh. In order that the pump might be tested and modified as necessary for possible use in other parts of the world the Mennonite Central Committee has not pursued a patenting right to the pump. However in spite of its extremely simplistic design and advantages such as ease of operation and straightforward fabrication, the pump has not been adopted extensively and has not passed into the domain of the informal entrepreneur.

The pump is nevertheless well known and is still widely used on tube-wells in Bangladesh where it is manufactured and sold locally by various producers and vendors. The original design has also been refined by Richard Cansdale of SWS Filtration who manufactures the pump and sells entire pumps or pump components that can be fitted into appropriate uPVC or ABS piping. The pump does have a number of advantages for the small-scale manufacturer as each pump has only a small number of components and no welding or complex fabrication equipment is required in the assembly.

Figure 7.1 shows the simplicity of a basic Rower pump.

Joma pumps

Simple components such as those used in the Rower pump may provide benefits for use in other applications. The Joma pump as shown in

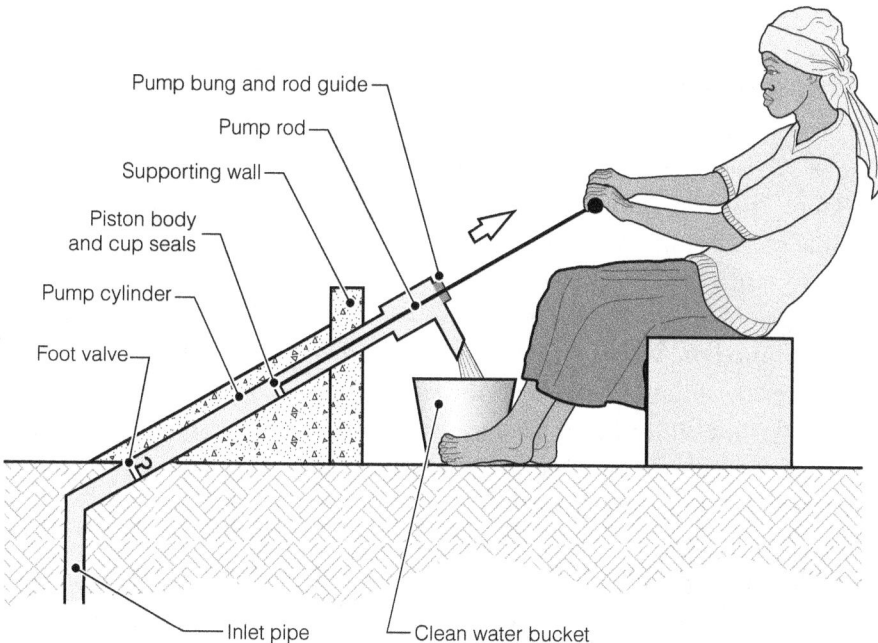

Labels: Pump bung and rod guide; Pump rod; Supporting wall; Piston body and cup seals; Pump cylinder; Foot valve; Inlet pipe; Clean water bucket

Figure 7.1. Rower pump

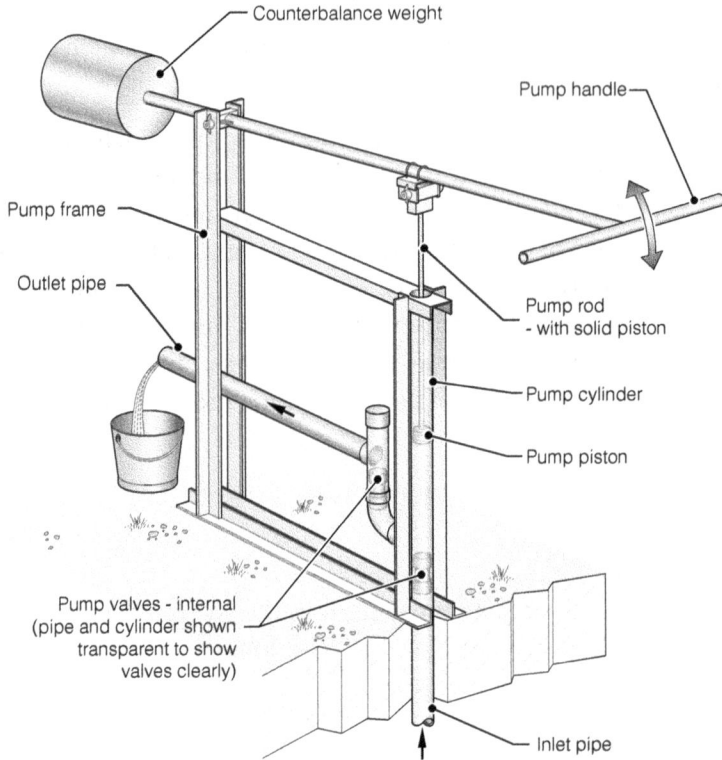

Figure 7.2. Joma pump

Figure 7.2 is a counterbalanced force type suction pump developed by Dabane Trust for use in conjunction with sand-abstraction systems. It is capable of drawing water from depths of 4 or 5 metres using atmospheric pressure and delivering water to a height of 6 to 8 metres. It has the advantage of being operated by two people simultaneously and uses simple Rower pump type valves and piston bodies. Sustained operating speeds of 30 strokes per minute have been measured and yields of 2.5 to 3.0m³ are regularly achieved. Figure 7.3 shows a simplistic representation of four handpumps that are suitable for sand-abstraction use, depending on the abstraction system to be used.

Treadle pumps

The Treadle pump also known as the Tapak pump was also designed for use in shallow groundwater applications in Bangladesh and can be used in similar situations to the Rower pump. However, whereas the Rower pump is a hand operated pump the treadle pump is leg operated and consequently as leg muscles are stronger than arm muscles, this design is less tiring to use and also has a higher potential output.

The pump has two cylinders and pistons that are joined into a single suction pipe. Above each cylinder is a beam that is hinged at one end and at the other connects to a piston. The beams have a cable which connects them and passes over a pulley. The operator stands with one foot on each beam and transfers weight first to one then to the other, thus as one piston goes down so the other comes up. The result is a very simple and very effective water pump.

There are two systems of pump available. One is a basic pump that can draw water from a depth and discharge it straight from the open top of the cylinders to flow by gravity directly into a low tank or open canal. The other is an enclosed cylinder system that can raise water to a height of up to 12 metres above the operating level.

Although the construction process of both Treadle pumps is more complex than the Rower pump, manufacture has been taken up by a number of small-scale industrial companies and many entrepreneurs in a number of countries produce the treadle pump for sale. Information on the principles of the pump and its construction can be gathered from books such as *How to Make and Use the Treadle Pump* which is available from Practical Action Publishing.

Rope and washer pumps

The Rope-and-washer pump is only suitable for installation on offset sand wells and collector wells that are fed by infiltration-galleries. Due to its particularly simple design and construction it is a handpump that can be produced relatively easily with no intricate equipment and only basic hand tools. There is a significant amount of experience in the use and reliability of this pump as a number of communities and service organizations use pumps that utilize this principle on shallow dug-wells.

Information is widely available on details of the pump and its construction from books and videos such as *How to Make a Rope Washer Pump* which are available from book vendors such as Practical Action Publishing.

Direct action pumps

Handpumps such as the commercially available Canzee and Tara pumps are suitable for use on offset sand wells and infiltration gallery collector wells due to their efficiency and general reliability. Because of their narrow-bore specifications they are particularly suitable for installation on tube-wells that draw water from shallow alluvial aquifers where the required lift is 6 to 15 metres.

Direct lift borehole pumps
Such as those in the India and Afridev ranges are best used in applications where there is a need to raise water from 20 to 100 metres rather than from the shallow lifts associated with sand-abstraction wells for which they are over-designed. However because of their widespread use and the general availability of spares such pumps might be considered for use on offset sand wells and infiltration gallery collector wells. These pumps can generally be purchased commercially but the design of pumps such as the India, the Afridev and the Bushpump, the Zimbabwean designed hand operated borehole pump, are each in the public domain.

Diaphragm pumps
Are akin to both the Rower and the Treadle pump in terms of installation, use and application. There are a number of designs of diaphragm pump and a variety of models, with manufacture occurring in several countries. Commercial models generally comprise a casting, to which a diaphragm, an inlet and an outlet valve are attached.

Unlike the Treadle and even the Rower pump, manufacture of the pump is not conducive to small-scale manufacture. The relatively large surface area and the distance through which a diagram is expected to flex makes for a point of weakness, particularly where a diaphragm is subjected to the additional pressure of raising water to a delivery head and may lead to rupture. Simplified designs of diaphragm pumps that use materials such as old car tyres tend to be as defective as they are effective.

Progressive cavity pumps
In handpump form are suitable for use on wells and tube-wells where the helical pump unit can be installed directly in water. They are particularly useful in high lift applications where water needs to be pumped to heights of above 10 metres.

Large-scale commercial systems

Progressive cavity pumps
Larger mechanically-powered pumps are also very suitable for sand-abstraction applications, particularly on multiple well-point and manifold systems. Surface operating progressive cavity pumps designed for horizontal use require a priming tank on the suction side of the pump with an approximate capacity 2½ times the combined volume of the manifold, connecting pipe and well-points. The top of the priming tank must be above

the top of the pump intake so that when full the pump will also contain water. The pump will draw water from the priming tank and in so doing reduce the air pressure in the tank to the extent that atmospheric pressure will, within the limits of pump efficiency and altitude, force water through the system. Water will then be conveyed from the well-points and manifold into the priming tank and pump from where it can be pumped away.

Although helical rotor and stator pumps have the ability to pump air it is imperative that both components remain lubricated with water at all times to prevent overheating to the detriment of the pump. The volume of the priming tank must be greater than that of the sealed system to ensure that there is sufficient water for the pump not to run dry before water is moving through all the pipework. On shut down the priming tank will require re-priming before the system can be used again.

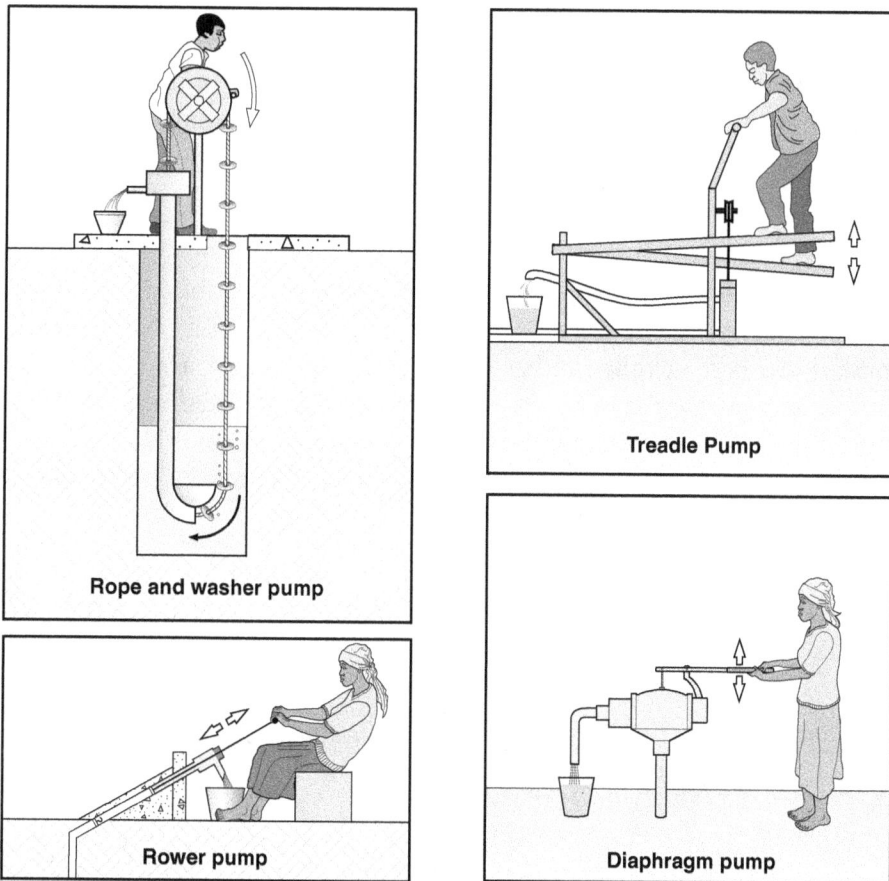

Figure 7.3. Handpumps suitable for sand-abstraction use

A progressive cavity borehole pump can be installed into a priming tank in much the same manner. A borehole pump requires installation in a sealed system that combines a pump casing/priming tank unit, a manifold and well-points. The priming tank is installed below the level of the manifold and also requires a capacity 2½ times the combined volume of the well-points, manifold and any connecting pipes. The borehole pump draws water from the priming tank which similarly reduces the air pressure in the tank so that atmospheric pressure will force water through the well-points and manifold into the priming tank from where it is pumped to the surface. Both Mono pump/Dresser and Orbit manufacture progressive cavity handpumps, deep well borehole pumps and horizontal water and sludge pumps.

Centrifugal pumps

High-speed mechanical pumps can be equipped for surface installation in the same situations that progressive cavity surface pumps can be installed. Centrifugal pumps do not have the same positive displacement attributes as progressive cavity pumps and are thus more efficient in installations that maintain as direct a connection as possible between the well-points and manifold and the priming tank.

Multi-stage submersible pumps

Electrically powered pumps are typically high yielding borehole pumps and are thus primarily suited for use on large-scale schemes. Submersible pumps are best installed either on collector wells that are charged by infiltration-galleries as in Ranney well systems or installed direct into large diameter well-screens where the rate of abstraction is lower than the rate of recharge and drawdown and where it can be assured that the system will not be damaged during river flow.

Photograph 7.1 shows the above ground level set up of three submersible borehole pumps that are installed in steel borehole casing that connect to manifolds and a matrix of well-points in a commercial scheme installed in the Limpopo River, Nottingham Estate, Beit Bridge, Zimbabwe.

A limited list of manufacturers of pumps suitable for sand-abstraction use is included in Appendix 2.

Table 7.1 provides an assessment of a typical range of static head, output, power requirement and efficiency of pumps that can be used to draw water from sand-abstraction systems. It can also be used in conjunction with Table 6.1 to help select the type of pump best suited to a specific abstraction system.

Photograph 7.1. Commercial tube-well and infiltration scheme using submersible pumps.

Table 7.2 provides a comparison of handpumps that are suitable for sand-abstraction use.

Pump operation and maintenance

Valves

A system is required that will keep water moving forward through a pump. A valve is a pump component that opens as water flows through in one direction but closes as the flow of water ceases. This allows water to move forward and not to move back in a pump. Valves may be opened and closed by the flow of water or by springs. The flaps that close the pipe may be made of flat brass or metal sheet, balls or hemi-spheres or rubber sheet.

Simple self-closing valves can be made from rubber sheet such as that used in vehicle inner tubes. Such material is easily obtained, is effective in low technology applications and is simple to fabricate for easy maintenance or repair.

Table 7.1. A typical range of static head, output, power requirement and efficiency of pumps

Operating system		Head range (m)	Flow range (m³/hr)	Input power (kW)	Efficiency (%)
Syphons		1 - 6			
Direct lift Pumps – Shallow well pumps	Bucket and Windlass	5 - 50	1	0.04 - 0.08	10 - 40
	Rope and washer	5 - 20	5 - 30	0.02 - 1	50 - 80
Displacement Pumps – Well and borehole pumps	Piston pumps	3 - 200+	1 - 100+	0.03 - 50+	40 - 85
	Diaphragm pump	1 - 2	2 - 20	0.03 - 5	20- 30
	Progressive cavity	10 - 100	2 - 100+	0.5 - 10	30 - 70
Velocity Pumps	Centrifugal	4 - 60	1 - 500+	0.1 - 500+	30 - 80
	Submersible	10 - 300	1 - 100	5 - 500+	30 - 80
	Jet pump	10 - 30	50 - 500	5 - 500+	20 - 60

Priming

Suction pumps work by removing air to create a vacuum so that atmospheric pressure can fill the subsequent void with water. As water is moved through the pump and piping so more water is drawn into and through the pump. However, a suction pump can only pump water and will not work when there is any air in the system. Even a small 'bubble' of air will mean that the pump is unable to move any water at all. As air can be compressed, so it can also expand, thus air in the system will inevitable mean that a suction pump will be unable to draw water through the pipes to be replaced by more water.

It is thus important to remove all air from a suction pump and replace it with water before pumping starts. It is also important to prevent any leaks that will allow air to be drawn into the pump and cause the flow of water to stop.

Type or trade name	Point of manufacture /repair	Operation	Appropriate use	Suitability
Rower	Village level assembly and repair	Rowing action	Well-points Collector well Offset sand well	Good
Treadle	Artisan workshop	Leg operated beams	Well-points Collector well Offset sand well	Good
Rope and Washer	Village level construction	Rotary	Collector well Offset sand well	Good
Canzee / Tara	Commercial	Direct action	Collector well Offset sand well	Good
Bucket	Artisan workshop	Windlass	Collector well Sand wells	Low yield
Blair bucket	Artisan workshop	Direct action	Collector well Sand wells	Low yield
Bush Pump	Commercial	Reciprocating piston	Collector well Offset sand well	Over designed Limited use
Afridev	Commercial	Reciprocating piston	Collector well Offset sand well	Over designed Limited use
Mono	Commercial	Hand operated rotary	Well-points Collector well Offset sand well	Good

Table 7.2. Handpump suitability

In order to optimize any power system, pump efficiency must be high. Any loss of water from the pump reduces the overall output or requires the power source to operate for longer periods or to pump more water in a given time. Ineffective or inefficient systems are wasteful of both the water resource and the operating system. To ensure efficiency it is imperative that the maximum volume of water is delivered in the shortest possible time allowed by the pump and power source.

Service and repair

Satisfactory operation and maintenance will also determine pump efficiency and an optimum supply of water. In order to ensure satisfactory performance a pump is required that is easy to operate, has few components and is simple and straightforward for end-users.

Although many pumps and maintenance systems are referred to as 'Village Level Operation and Maintenance' (VLOM), for such a system to be effective it is imperative that the following points are agreed on:

- Suitable rules and regulations for effective management and user responsibilities. Agreements should cover; quantities of water that can be drawn at any one time, when water can be drawn, the use to which water can be put and who can draw water.
- Suitable people will need to be identified and trained in pump operation and maintenance. Training appropriate to the water supply and the abstraction and pump technology must be provided.
- Agreements will be required as to who will pay for maintenance and/or repair materials and who will undertake the work. If pump users are not prepared to contribute in cash or kind to maintenance/repair work even the most reliable water supply facility will ultimately become a failure.
- A comprehensive supply of 'fast-moving' spares will need to be assembled and stored or a reliable supplier or manufacturer of spares identified

Power options

Pumps require power and as with the pumps themselves, there are a number of systems that can be applied:

- Human energy – usually referred to as hand-pumps
  - Activated by hand and body
  - Activated by leg
    Direct, walking action
    Cycling, chain or gears
- Animal-powered engines
- Fuel powered engines
- Electric motors
  - Mains electricity
  - Solar energy

Human power

The most basic method of operating a pump is by 'hand', effecting movement on a pump piston by way of a rod and handle. This can be either direct (direct lift) for low lift/low volume pumps or with a mechanical advantage through a fulcrum and pivot or a rotating wheel (direct action). Each system uses the relatively small muscles of the arms and back and can be very tiring.

A more efficient method is to use the larger leg muscles of the human body. A reciprocating action can be achieved through a walking motion, as in the treadle pump and rotary motion through the use of a crank and pedals with a chain wheel and gears. A useful mechanical advantage is achieved through pedal power and is used to drive appliances such as small grain grinding or plate mills. Although not commonly used to power pumps the system could be used in rotary applications such as progressive cavity pumps.

Hand power is a simple and straightforward pumping procedure. Little or no training or skill is required to operate a handpump system and there is little financial cost. There are no equipment purchase and installation costs and no apparent fuel, service/maintenance costs. With no obvious technical constraints and low financial operating costs, sustainability is generally high.

The disadvantages of handpump systems are a low output of water, the comparatively hard work required to maintain continuous pumping and the long periods of time needed for pumping which reduces the time available for other ventures and responsibilities. To compound this, human muscle power is inefficient in the conversion of the calories obtained in food into kW's of energy produced.

Although during short, strenuous periods muscle efficiency may be as high as 20-30% which compares favourably with an internal combustion engine, the continuous daily muscular work capability of a person is approximately 0.2 to 0.3kWhr/day, which is a low 7-11% efficiency of food energy conversion to mechanical energy. Thus although commonly used, human muscular energy is not cheap. People with a low income are forced to use human power as the actual cash investment is low and many are unable to afford anything else, however almost any other source of power will, volume for time, pump water more cheaply. As human work output is only some 0.25kW/day it will require four days work by one person to produce 1kW, which equates to the output of a small engine in an hour. Only when factoring in other costs and considerations such as procurement and the availability of fuel and spares and the power requirement for the generally low yields of water that are required does human power become acceptable at a community water supply level. At a higher output commercial farming level human-powered pumps are not viable.

Improvements to the efficiency of human power can be made through ergonomics and the use of selected muscles in a suitable action at a correct speed through a light but strong mechanism. The human body exerts 50% more power by pedalling, utilising the legs than by pushing a handle up and down with the arms. Dynamometer tests indicate that the average cyclist works at 0.75kW when cycling at 18km/hr, if this output is fully utilized in pumping, the flow rates in Table 7.3 could be achieved.

As they are powered by larger leg muscles, foot or leg operated pumps are considered more effective for irrigation than hand or arm operated pumps and as irrigation pumps require operation for several hours a day such efficiency is crucial. However, acceptability and operator's personal preferences for pump action must also be considered, as well as the pump application. Hand operated devices may be more convenient to use than leg operated pumps thus it may be more appropriate to use smaller pumps with a lighter action to pump smaller quantities of water over a longer period of time.

The criteria for defining a good human-powered irrigation pump to pump a relatively large volume of water are likely to be significantly different from those for a suitable low volume domestic water supply pump. Thus consideration of the pump requirement, as well as the pumping method is important in the selection of a suitable manually operated pump. The efficiency of hand pumping may be improved through the use of counterbalance weights, such as shown in Figure 7.2, which are able to adjust a pump to the proportion of energy required between drawing water into the pump, and discharging it.

Figure 7.4 indicates the basic handpump actions and typical pumping preferences.

Table 7.3. Pumping rates that can be theoretically achieved by pedal power					
Pumping head (m)	0.5	1.0	2.5	5.0	10.0
Delivery (m³/hr)	27.5	13.8	5.5	2.2	1.1
World Water magazine					

Reciprocating handpump actions

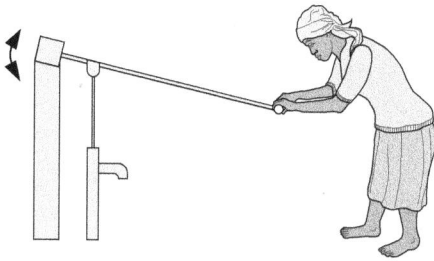

Disliked action   Preferred action

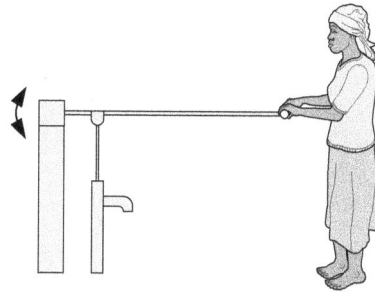

Rotary handpump actions

Disliked action   Preferred action

Figure 7.4.   Handpump actions and pumping preferences

Animal power

The use of animal-powered 'engines' declined with the advent of the steam engine and the internal combustion engine. Because there was limited demand for large quantities of water when animal-powered engines were in widespread use there was little application made of them for driving displacement type water pumps. However pumps such as the continuous rope and washer, the Persian wheel and water scoop wheels have long been animal-powered.

The use of animals to pump water is appropriate in remote dryland areas where engines and fuel are both expensive and difficult to obtain. However, in order to optimize the efficiency of draught animals, additional fodder may be required.

Capstan, rotated by harnessing to a donkey

Priming valve

Car pick-up tyre,
acting as diaphragm
pump, being moved in
and out by pitman

Crank, turned
by the capstan

Outlet valve and
delivery pipe

Scotch yoke,
turned by crank

Pitman or con rod,
moved in and out
by scotch yoke

All bearings made
from hardwood

Angle iron frame

Fixed plate

Well

Inlet valve and pipe

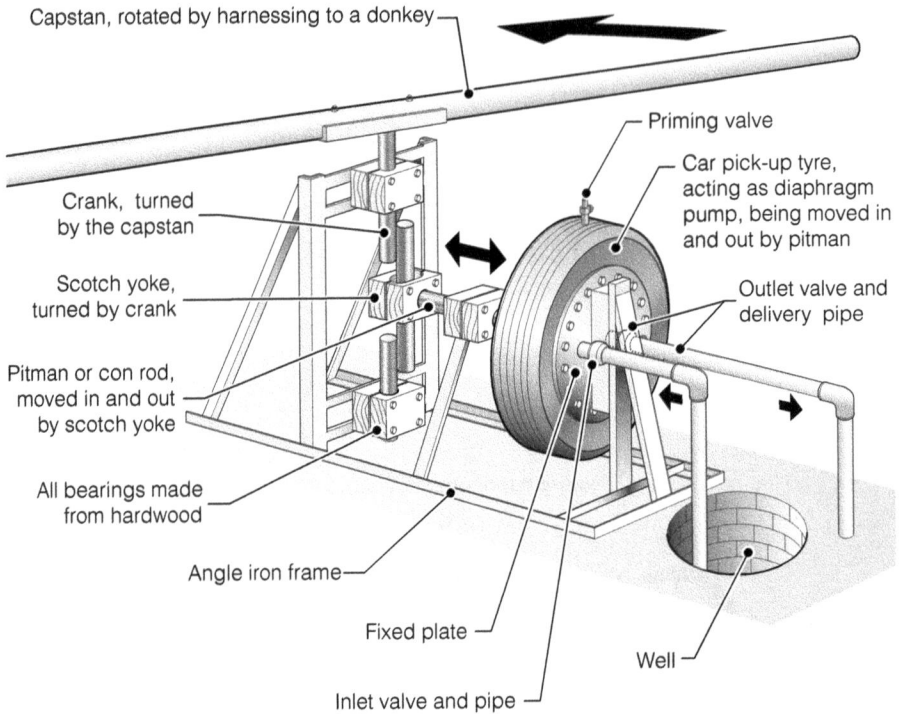

Figure 7.5. Experimental animal-powered diaphragm pump

Although the increasing availability of relatively low-cost, 'throw-away' stationary engines means that animal power is seldom used, opportunities do exist to use animals to drive pumps. The slow moving diaphragm pump in particular is suited to animal power applications. Figure 7.5 shows an experimental animal-powered diaphragm pump that uses a car or pick-up tyre that is sealed with steel plates. A crank which is turned by two donkeys extends and retracts a pitman that increases and decreases the interior volume of the tyre, drawing water in as it expands and pumping out as it contracts. Unfortunately in this model the rotation is so slow, approximately only 3.3 r.p.m, that the valves do not bed sufficiently accurately to maintain an airtight seal and the prime is quickly lost.

Internal combustion engines

There is presently little demand for steam engines or for external combustion engines. Due to its versatility the internal combustion engine is probably the most commonly used source of power for pumping water. Piston engines can be used to power pumps whether the requirement is rotary or reciprocating and can be used in any sand-abstraction application. Engines range in size from small <1kW portable self-priming pump/petrol engine units to large diesel engines of several hundred kW that provide fixed power to multiple well-point systems capable of irrigating hundreds of hectares.

Motorized self-priming centrifugal pump units are capable of making handy and efficient small-scale irrigation and livestock water systems. Small petrol or diesel engine pumps, stationary or portable, coupled to one or several well-points sunk into the river alluvium provide a simple and effective system of water abstraction. Such units are able to pump significantly larger volumes of water with considerably greater ease of operation and without tedium than can be supplied by hand pumping.

The disadvantage is the increased cost of operation and maintenance, which is considerably compounded where there are problems associated with obtaining fuel and service materials. A knowledgeable and skilled operator is required as is a competent mechanic to undertake the service and repair of the unit. The sustainability of engine powered pump units is often questionable and there is sometimes the added drawback that small engines may be stolen

Large, fixed plant schemes with large engines are capable of providing high volumes of water over long distances or to great heights if required. As with smaller engine powered units, operation is easy and requires little physical effort. However, although larger volumes of water can be pumped, such systems are expensive to operate and maintain. Supplies of fuel and service materials can be a real problem and a competent mechanic is certainly required.

Electric motors

Where either mains electricity or series of solar panels are available electric motors may be used in any application where an internal combustion engine can be used. As with internal combustion units, motor/pump units range from very low output to very large output systems

As with all fast moving machinery, any exposed shafts, pulleys and belts require safety guards. In addition, electric motors, if not properly safeguarded, have the further limitation of potentially lethal electricity.

Wind power

Wind power has relatively little application with sand-abstraction systems. Windpumps are dependent on the velocity of the wind in relation to the size and efficiency of the rotor, the volume of water to be pumped and the pumping heads. Consequently wind power is only practical on collector well and offset sand well systems where pump priming is not required. A further limitation is that wind speeds tend to be reduced in valley bottoms where sand-abstraction systems are located.

Table 7.4 indicates the advantages and disadvantages of four distinct power systems.

Table 7.4. Pump power systems		
Application	**Advantage**	**Disadvantage**
Human or hand power	• Simple and straight-forward • Little or no financial outlay to operate • Low maintenance costs and not difficult to repair	• Inefficient - poor return on inputs • Can be hard work – long and tiring • Mechanically inefficient, may be frequent breakdowns
Animal power	• Animals work for a longer period of time than humans – more cost effective • Not complex, low maintenance costs and not difficult to repair	• Animals may require additional feed • Technology not commonly used or understood
Internal combustion engines	• Both engines and power transfer systems widely available • Efficient pumping for a protracted period of time	• Costly in outlay and in operating, service/maintenance, repair and replacement costs • Inputs; fuel, oil, spares may be costly or difficult to obtain • Skilled operator required
Electric motors	• Efficient • Can be used by unskilled operators	• Limited to availability of mains electricity or solar panel displays • Efficiency impaired where there is intermittent power supply or over-cast weather
Wind power	• Low running costs – although maintenance is required	• Not suited to widespread use • Costly, windmills tend to be as expensive to purchase as internal combustion engines • Suitable sites may be difficult to find

Hand powered pumps are suitable for:

- Low-cost, low volume requirements
- VLOM systems that are relatively easily maintained and repaired
- small-scale rural/community water supplies

Animal-powered pumps are suitable for:

- low-technology pumping applications
- low lift applications
- some application with some pumps designed primarily for use with internal combustion engine/electric motor power

Engine and electric motor powered pumps are suitable for:

- fixed plant equipment (engine pump and base) schemes
- commercial water supply systems –
  - domestic, livestock and irrigation schemes
  - commercial farms, ranches and irrigation schemes
  - supplies to towns

Chapter summary

An appraisal is made of the suitability of specific pumps for both small-scale community based sand-abstraction systems and larger scale commercial systems. Simple suction pumps are generally the most suitable and versatile pumps as they are simple to operate, relatively straightforward to service and repair and are generally suited to all small-scale sand-abstraction pumping requirements.

The principle of suitable pumps is explained together with appropriate sources of operating power. Full VLOM systems of pump operation and maintenance are advocated with end users being encouraged to accept complete responsibility for pump operation, service and repair systems. As one of the advantages of basic sand-abstraction is the simplicity of the system, ideally rural communities should be encouraged to undertake well-point and handpump fabrication and installation work for themselves.

It has to be acknowledged that technical solutions are only a part of the answer. As well as the relatively straightforward process of selecting a suitable abstraction and pump system if an independent, long-lasting, community sustainable water supply scheme is to be ensured it is imperative that consideration be given to the difficult issue of ownership and responsibility for equipment.

8

Social aspects

IN THIS CHAPTER:
The identification of social problems that communities will need to resolve in order to establish enduring, independent and sustainable water supplies. These include:
- Considerations of culture – Established perceptions and existing management systems:
  - Access to water – Who gets to use the water?
  - Gender and technology – Who controls the technology, the use of water and the quantities that can be drawn?
- Responsibility and ownership – Who is responsible for the supply and who accepts ownership of the pump?
  - How much water may each person draw each day?
  - For what purpose may the water be used?
  - How much are people prepared to pay or contribute for the upkeep of the water supply?
- Operation and maintenance regimes – Effective maintenance/repair training
  - Who will participate and how many people will undergo pump maintenance training?
  - Who has the authority to pump water and who will undertake maintenance/repair work on the pump?

Making community water schemes work

The sociological aspects of a community water supply are without doubt most critical to the success of an independent scheme. It is relatively straightforward to produce a technical solution, but much more complex to achieve a sociological solution that will ensure a permanent water supply. If the users are not in agreement on the management of a source of water and do not contribute or work together to operate and maintain it, the system will not remain operational in the long term. It is imperative that critical issues of operation and maintenance should be identified and that communities discuss and resolve these issues in order to establish an enduring, independent and sustainable water supply.

If a source of water is to provide an on-going supply, communities cannot merely accept a system and expect either centralized maintenance/repair services or an implementing agency or donor to keep the supply operational. The initiation of a community water supply is invariably driven by services external to the community – whether they are conceived as a part of a national plan or through donor agency sponsorship. Whilst this may provide an immediate water supply solution, the abstraction and pump system will not be a lasting solution unless the users recognize their right to clean water and their responsibility to maintain it. No system will be sustainable unless the community is able to manage the system for itself. This means that all users must be prepared to take responsibility and to contribute to the operation, maintenance and repair of abstraction equipment. To this end, to ensure that everyone will adhere to decisions made, there must be a transparent decision-making process, even if the final decision is delegated to an elected committee.

Agreements and rules must be developed in regard to use, operation and maintenance/repair systems. This is particularly difficult where water is being abstracted from a communal water supply as no agreement will be achieved if there is not first agreement on the quantity of water that can be drawn by a family and the use that can be made of the water.

Photograph 8.1. Community meeting

A sustainable water supply will not be achieved by providing the hardware alone. More important than an immediate technical solution is a lasting sociological solution

Rules and regulations, important as they are, are useful only as long as they are supported and agreed by all the end users. There is little point in preparing agreements or constitutions if they are not popularly supported and thus unlikely to be followed.

For those engaged in community work, probably the most positive approach is to cultivate an atmosphere of dialogue and openness amongst the users. Only by acceptance and consideration of all issues, as they might apply to the entire community will there be any likelihood of common agreement leading to systems and strategies that will ensure a long and productive water supply.

Photograph 8.1 shows an informal community meeting led by staff of Dabane Trust discussing the water supply problem at Siyachilaba, Binga District, Zimbabwe.

Cultural perceptions, traditions and gender

Perceptions and management

Because of the need to preserve life in many societies in dryland areas where water is typically in short supply it is a traditional perception that no one should be refused access to water. However, the establishment of present-day infrastructure can no longer support this principle.

Water cannot be assumed to be 'free for all'. Costs are undoubtedly incurred in any mechanized system, no matter how simple, from straightforward maintenance and repair costs to operator and running costs and possibly the payment of water authority levies.

Long-established customs in the primary use of water may also persist today. Particularly where water reserves are limited difficulties frequently arise between those who traditionally consider that preference should be given to livestock as users of secondary water and those who wish to use water for irrigation. Altercations can also arise between those who are of the opinion that there should be a flat rate for all users and those who make little use of the water and invariably expect those who make much use of the water to contribute appreciably more.

The use of water and responsibility for equipment is particularly important where water supplies are limited or where some members, but not all of the community operate water-based projects. Rules and regulations on quantities of water and the time when water can be drawn must be recognized and agreed on by the entire community and all those who wish to benefit from water related development schemes.

Invariably the expectation of a community based scheme will not only be for an improved water supply but also for an increased supply of water – broadly the anticipation will be water-for-all and for all purposes. The hopes are that there will be plenty of water for household use, in addition to water for livestock and for irrigation. Consequently, unless controls or limitations are placed on the use or quantities of water that can be drawn, a source of water may not last throughout an entire dry-season.

A community in an area where the groundwater drawn from boreholes was badly contaminated by mineral salts worked together to develop a source of water from sand-abstraction. The supply was not plentiful but it was clean and highly palatable. As a result people came from far and wide and from beyond the immediate community in order to draw such appealing water. They also came with donkey carts and large drums to the extent that demand exceeded supply. In order to maintain the supply agreements had to be reached on whom, when and how much water could be drawn at any one time.

In many societies it is a common sentiment that water is 'God-given, and therefore 'free'. Considerable division and dispute can arise within a community if not everyone is prepared to work for and accept responsibility for a source of water.

Typically, over a period of time, communities have evolved traditional management and use systems for seasonal and alternate water supplies that have no infrastructure. The management systems for these are often based around use by a group of close families or a clan within the greater community. Where relationships are already established and people have an innate trust of each other and the experience and tradition of working together, it may well be possible to develop these existing management systems and perceptions to the benefit of a new small-scale water supply scheme.

Gender – responsibility and use of water

In many societies responsibility for the provision of water for domestic purposes rests with women. It is a traditional taboo that men and boys

Free water?

The Dabane Trust worked with villagers at Dongamuzi, Lupane District, Zimbabwe to construct an earth embankment dam. Almost everyone within the community assisted with collecting rock and building materials and loading and unloading trailers, collecting water, consolidating the embankment, digging foundations, mixing building mortar, stone pitching the embankment and any number of support tasks to improve the dam and catchment area and to keep the equipment operating. When the dam was complete and the first water held in the basin, people brought their few cattle and livestock to drink. One particular cattle owner came with a huge herd. The community queried the right of this person to use the dam as he had not participated in the construction work and had sent no member of his family to assist. His response was that whilst he accepted that the dam belonged to the community and not to him, the water was *'God given' and free for the use of everyone*.......

should not be seen carrying water, although it is generally acceptable for them to collect water in drums by donkey cart. Where there is the possibility, many men prefer to water their cattle and small livestock at a dam rather than from a groundwater and handpump supply. Thus it is that men tend to visit handpump water supplies infrequently and may have little or no knowledge or interest in the operation and management of a domestic water supply.

As a result there are differing opinions between men and women on the use and requirements of water supply equipment. Consequently men generally have little incentive to maintain water supply systems, unless they have a direct need of the water. This has a negative impact on the maintenance and repair of equipment as generally women do not have access to independent funds to repair pump infrastructure and thus there is not the investment in maintenance and repairs that there should be.

To compound this situation, men often become interested in a source of water only if there is a significant technological development, such as an engine associated with the scheme. Men then wish to manage the scheme but frequently have little or no experience in water source use and either dominate the scheme so that women are unfairly disadvantaged or over-use and over-abstract water to the detriment of the scheme and the overall supply of water to the community.

Figure 8.1 indicates a group of women who have the management and control of their own water supply system rejecting the suggestion to upgrade their pump.

Baobab magazine

Figure 8.1. Accepting responsibility for a water supply

In areas of water shortage there is often a clash of interest between those who wish to use water for livestock and those who wish to use water for irrigation. This division often manifests itself on lines of gender. Men wish to keep livestock, often for status and ceremonial purposes rather than for food security or financial reasons, and women wish to have the direct use of water for food production for the family.

Particularly in areas of water shortage it is a common practice that a household will draw water from 3 or 4 sources in order to maintain 'a stake' in each where their presence is seen and where they are accepted. If one system is not working then there is a known, alternative supply and

A young man with no mechanical training prevented a group of 15 women from effectively operating their engine-powered pump unit and garden by insisting that he was the technical expert and the only one competent within the community to operate the engine – frequently with disastrous results. The women felt unable to challenge him so that in effect he high-jacked the scheme. By controlling the technology and totally restricting access, the women were completely dependent on him. Consequently the group only had irrigation water when he provided it and his lack of knowledge and mechanical ability increased breakdowns and decreased the financial income of the group.

The need for a number of sources of water to be available to one family and the cause of community water supply breakdowns may not always be immediately apparent. In the process of repairing a community handpump in the Tsholotsho District of Zimbabwe, a series of questions to a number of young girls unravelled an unusual response.

The pump which was being upgraded to a garden water supply was found to be full of small stones. Asked why this was, the girls replied shyly that they frequently dropped small stones inside the pump column because they liked to hear the sound the stones made as they ricocheted down the steel pipe. In response to the obvious statement that it was because of this that the pump had ceased to operate, their reply was that the breakdown was an added advantage as they then had to walk further to fetch water and so they then had less work to do during the day as they could justifiably stay longer away from home!

the option exists to draw water from another source. In fact it is often the case that when an abstraction system is not operative, rather than attend to the breakdown, both women and men will simple use an alternative source even if it is considerably further afield.

Issues such as these may present implementing organizations with a dilemma, whom should they be working with? Is it best to work with communities that are well organized and who demonstrate a wish to develop their own, improved water supply and are likely to make a success of it but who are ostensibly more affluent? Alternatively should development agencies undertake their work with communities that obviously have a need but are less organized, more divided and may be apathetic and without the motivation of the better established communities and are thus less likely to succeed?

Responsibility and ownership

Throughout the industrially developing world there is a plethora of broken down infrastructure and failed development initiatives which have occurred simply because responsibility and ownership have not been understood or accepted. Until these issues have been discussed and agreed on, no one will be prepared to contribute to the maintenance or repair of equipment that they feel they may lose the use of.

Too often a water supply is viewed as the responsibility of the donor and belonging to the implementing agency. Until this perception is confronted and end-users are able to accept responsibility for a water supply the likelihood of a continuing scheme is poor.

The establishment of ownership and responsibility is thus vital. Without an effective management system and with the users not aware of the need for one, or not prepared for the responsibility, the beneficiaries will simply revert to existing or traditional systems, even if considerably more inconvenient and abandon any new equipment. With no agreement the community or clan will not feel sufficiently confident to take responsibility for infrastructure. The sentiment likely to be expressed to an implementing agency will be – 'your pump has failed me'.

The use of water and responsibility for equipment is particularly important where water is in short supply or where some members, but not all of the community, operate water-based projects. Rules and regulations on quantities of water and the time when water can be drawn must be recognized and agreed on by the entire community and all those who wish to benefit from water related development schemes. Photograph 8.2 shows a water-point committee discussing water-point management with members of the community.

Constraints to responsible ownership

- Former centralized systems which were used to carry out routine maintenance and repair work with no apparent cost to a community. With this legacy communities are now reluctant to contribute to decentralized maintenance repair systems.

Photograph 8.2. Water-point committee holding discussions with the community

Christian Aid / L. Orton

- Stakeholders reluctant to make an investment or to donate funds or materials to repair equipment, for fear that it cannot be repaired or may be removed for major repair and ultimately not replaced.
- Concern regarding the cost of maintaining equipment.
- Poorly managed maintenance systems where repair equipment or spares are not available, maintenance or repair work is sub-standard or contributions are mishandled.

Possible solutions

The fore-going can usually be distilled as need for a system that people are prepared to operate and maintain themselves, which they feel they can afford to maintain and which they understand. The following will provide a basis from which solutions can be developed:

- Low-cost, low-tech water supply systems that do not require specialist repair tools and are simple and cheap to maintain.
- A constitution or code of ethics developed by the community on issues relating to the water-point and the operation, maintenance and repair of equipment. Implementation of the agreement and penalties imposed on those in breach of agreements.

Table 8.1 is the format of a basic constitution developed by Dabane Trust that is modified through discussion with community groups to meet the requirement of a particular group of users.

Table 8.5 at the end of this chapter is a constitution translated from the vernacular that the Bekezela Garden group has drawn up for their own use. The garden is in Nkashe Village, Gwanda District, Matabeleland South, Zimbabwe. It should be noted the agreement addresses the topics shown in Table 8.1 as considered by the group. It is not a definitive, legal and binding agreement but is an agreement that has been thrashed out by the group and is expressed in a form that is acceptable to themselves and thus has a greater likelihood of being adhered to.

Water supply management

In order to ensure a sustainable water supply for which people accept responsibility it is important that equable agreement be reached on matters of management. Matters that must be addressed are:

- How many people and which members of the community are able to make use of the water supply.
- The purpose for which water may be used.

WATER FROM SAND RIVERS

Table 8.1.	Format for a governing document for groups supported by Dabane Trust

Constitution
1. Name of Project/Group/Community 2. Address 3. Physical address 4. Contact person 5. Goal 6. Objectives 7. Membership 8. Office bearers – duties – term of office 9. Operational task 10. Working relationships 11. Banking 12. Safeguarding infrastructure 13. Meetings 14. Bye laws 15. Arbitration/disciplinary committee 16. Amendment of constitution 17. Vows Name ID No. Signature

- How much water each person may draw each day.

- What the water will cost. Who sets the levy or tithe payable, to whom payments are made, where investments are made and signatories to accounts.

- Who is authorized to purchase pump spares and who has custody of pump components and spares and pump maintenance and repair equipment.

- Who has the authority to pump water.

- Who should be trained in pump maintenance and who is responsible for carrying out maintenance and repair work on the pump.

Although responsibility for providing water, keeping water clean and generally maintaining a water supply system have traditionally been devolved to women, fuller participation and decision making is usually barred to women due to other traditional beliefs regarding the roles of men and women in society. At the household and community level it is men who make the decisions and consequently in many developing countries women are not involved in initial planning. Women are perceived as water providers and as a result very few receive technical training and are not encouraged to maintain pump equipment.

Constraints to effective management

Many of the decisions that must be made on the management and sustainability of a new water-point will not be easily reached. It is more than likely that that most of the users will expect a maximum amount of water at a minimum cost. With little experience in pump maintenance and repair, costing and budgeting and little surplus income it is more than likely that the levies set will be unrealistically low. Even reaching agreement on a levy will be a difficult decision for a community operating an efficient, brand new pump.

There can be obstinate malcontents in any community who often oppose the general trend, either due to a vested interest or for little more reason than self aggrandisement.

Possible solutions

- The establishment of a popularly elected committee that is sanctioned to implement agreements that will manage the water-point, whose decisions people will respect. Although meeting the aspirations of everyone within the community will be virtually impossible, the more that issues are discussed, the greater will be the success of the scheme and the likelihood of sustainability.

- Capacity building and training for members of the community who are critical to the scheme. The introduction of any technical development or development of infrastructure should be accompanied with capacity building and appropriate training provided to end-users.

Capacity building is essential to ensure that those who will use the water supply appreciate the need for effective management that will ensure sustainability.

- Each and every user of the water supply should understand the method of electing committee members, of reaching agreement and of adopting procedures.

- Efforts should be made to ensure that everyone appreciates the importance of appointing the most suitable and most competent person for the job and of overcoming vested interests when these are contrary to the sustainability of the scheme.

- Agreement must be reached on decisions relating to the management of the water supply and the need for equitable methods of utilising the water resource. As far as possible everyone should understand and agree with the decisions that are adopted, or alternatively should accept the limitations and penalties that can be imposed if in dissent.

It is important that everyone within the community is aware of all that is required to operate and maintain a successful water supply, the limitations of the supply and implications of poor management and leadership. The establishment of an effective water-point committee that is able to implement decisions and operate the water supply in the best interests of the community is an essential element of successful operation and maintenance. However it must be appreciated that any water-point committee will invariably be presented with many diverse demands and objections to their decisions and authority. A community or group that has a common purpose and a degree of unity will invariably have a greater chance of succeeding and maintaining a permanent water supply than a disorganized and disparate group.

A satisfactory management system may be difficult to achieve. Whilst specific skills training can be effectively provided in pump maintenance and repair this is not the case with community capacity building – either one has leadership skills or one does not. Of a survey of sand-abstraction water-points undertaken in 2003 (Table 7.2) 26% of the gardens reported an operational difficulty of one sort or another and of these 78% indicated that the problem was of a non-technical nature.

Operation and maintenance

There are three principle pump and water supply maintenance systems - centralized, partly centralized and de-centralized. Depending on the number of installations and the level of service required, the resources available and the water supply/maintenance policies of a country or region each system has its advantages and disadvantages.

Community groups most likely to succeed will exhibit:

- A common interest – an understanding and agreement to work together.
- Commitment – determined people will take the initiative, do things for themselves and not wait around for things to happen.
- Experience in working together - prior involvement in a club or activity that has already brought them together.
- Support from the greater community – a group or project working against the common will, will not succeed.
- An ability to listen and/or evaluate technical instruction and advice.

Table 8.2. Dabane Trust 2003 survey

Survey of irrigated gardens	No.	%
Total number of gardens surveyed	105	100
Gardens experiencing little or no operational problems	78	74
Gardens experiencing operational problems	27	26
Gardens with a technical problem	6	22
Gardens with a sociological problem	21	78

1. **Centralized system.** A fully centralized system undertakes responsibility for all water supply and system maintenance and repair needs of a community. Decisions on priority areas and communities, where to access and provide water, when and what to service/repair, are all undertaken by personnel exterior to the local community. Although service and maintenance can be undertaken regularly in rotation, breakdowns pose a problem and have to be attended to separately. Invariably such systems are expensive to operate with staff on call travelling from a central position when the need arises. Communities have no control over their water supply, spares and repair equipment are not available locally and no local person has the skill, the training or authority to service or repair equipment.

2. **Partially decentralized system.** This system generally has one or more members of the community trained in pump maintenance and repair. In an effective system one person, often referred to as a 'pump minder' has the responsibility for maintaining several water-points and has a team of assistants from within the community. Spares and service and maintenance equipment can be drawn from a central supply or are available locally and professional assistance can be called on in the event of a problem beyond the scope of the local maintenance team.

   A partially decentralized system might appear to have the advantages of both the centralized and the decentralized system. However in reality fast moving spares are often not available and maintenance/repair equipment which should be held at the village level can be far from the breakdown, or worse, cannot be found.

3. **Fully decentralized scheme.** This system is operated totally by the local community. Such a system is typically referred to as a village level operation and maintenance scheme, (VLOM). In its ultimate state the local community is entirely responsible for all operation,

maintenance and repair work. To be reliable and fully effective this requires appropriate equipment that a community with few skills and resources will be able to maintain and repair.

Ideally a VLOM system should be fully maintained and repaired with locally available tools and from materials that are readily available to the community. However many professionals still regard a system as VLOM, provided the users are able to obtain manufactured spares and equipment from an available source and to effect repairs for themselves.

In spite of often-limited community resources and skills a VLOM system will generally provide a more reliable water supply than a non-VLOM system as indicated in Table 8.3.

Important factors include which people and how many will be provided with pump maintenance and repair training. The more people who are trained the greater the likelihood of the community solving the problem and effecting a successful pump repair, however the position of a responsible water-point committee may then be undermined and responsible use generally less clearly defined.

Where there is a limited number of users a possible alternative is to place responsibility for pump maintenance and repair with a small core group but to provide training to everyone in the group. Table 8.4 indicates the success achieved with four training options adopted by the Dabane Trust over a ten year period from 1995 to 2005.

The success of a water supply project will ultimately come down to the ability of a community to develop a workable management system, the best an outsider to the community can do is to make people aware of the likely problems.

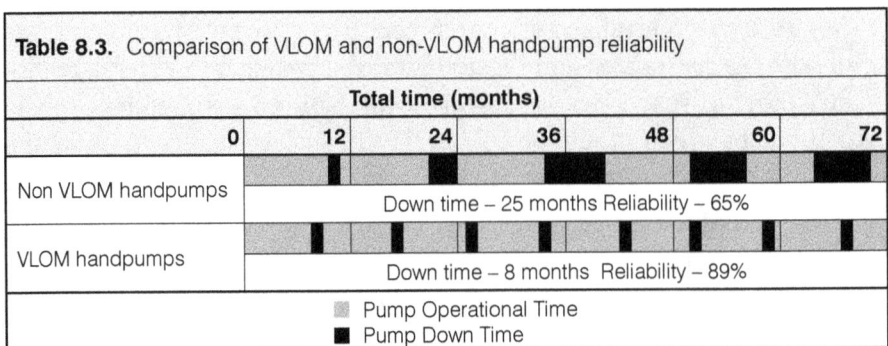

Table 8.3. Comparison of VLOM and non-VLOM handpump reliability

Total time (months)						
0	12	24	36	48	60	72

Non VLOM handpumps	Down time – 25 months Reliability – 65%
VLOM handpumps	Down time – 8 months Reliability – 89%

▨ Pump Operational Time
■ Pump Down Time

A problem frequently associated with non-working handpumps is the reluctance of the users to make regular payment for equipment maintenance. This may be due to:

- Non-availability of spares or sub-standard spares
- Insufficient or inadequate tools to effect satisfactory repairs
- Inexperienced pump minders providing poor quality repair/maintenance service or workmanship
- Pump minders over-charging
- Inadequate or poor collection of maintenance funds, misappropriated or badly managed systems of financing
- Other considerations are the cost of initial installation and more importantly the cost of repair, reliability and typical down time before equipment is brought back into service
- Inability to pay – Child headed households and those headed by old or terminally sick people have very little available finance

Table 8.4. Pump maintenance/repair options for a 15 – 20 member group

	Options	Success
1	No one trained	Minimum success
2	3 members trained	Good
3	Everyone trained	Better
4	Everyone trained with 3 responsible	Best

There is no single or guaranteed method of ensuring acceptance of all that is required of a community to ensure a sustainable, long-lasting water supply system. The best that can be done is to make each community aware of the complexity of successful water supply management and of the pitfalls likely to be associated with the operation and responsibility of equipment which one may use, but not own.

The best solution to such a situation is openness and negotiation. However, it is all too easy to simplify a solution. In their attempts to ensure success, development workers are sometimes guilty of offering solutions expecting them to work, and when they don't, either blaming the beneficiaries or themselves!

The Dabane Trust has found that women invariably have a better aptitude for repairing simple handpumps than men. Although training is provided to all participants of a water-point and garden group it is the all-women groups that have achieved the better maintenance/repair rate. This has been ascribed to women wanting to understand the pump, paying attention during training sessions and then when confronted with a technical problem, getting together, discussing and sharing ideas to work through the problem successfully.

However, the Dabane training team reports that in mixed groups, because of a perceived male technical talent, the women tend to leave the training to the men who inevitably pay little attention as they consider the pumps very simple and easy to fix. Unfortunately, when there is a breakdown, many men do not have the ability to effect a repair and consequently the water supply suffers.

The 'community car'

It can be all too easy to prescribe a water supply management solution from a handbook or from the security of an office.

To put in context problems associated with managing a 'community asset' such as a community handpump, particularly for people who are not a part of a resource-poor community, it may be beneficial to think through the following:

Imagine a housing estate in an industrial country (the community) where no one has a car. A car is donated to the residents by a local car dealership. Now imagine the process of ensuring that everyone has equal access and deciding who gets to use it: when; how often; at what cost; who is responsible for it; who fuels it; where; who attends to breakdowns; who pays for them; and what to do when inevitably the management system collapses!

Table 8.5. A discussed and agreed list of rules and regulations translated from the vernacular

Constitution	
Name:	Bekezela Garden.
Address:	Nkashe School, P.O Box 97, Gwanda.
Area / Place:	Nkashe Village, Ward 1, Mat South.
Contact Person:	Mr Richard Mpofu.
Goal:	Our aim is to plant / grow as much as possible, harvest and sell so that we can all get something.
Ways of achieving our goal (objective):	We are looking at planting all types of vegetables such as rape, onions, carrots, cabbage, spinach, beans, choumolia, and okra.
Being a member:	1. You must be resident of Nkashe. 2. There can only be one (1) member per family. 3. You must not be formally employed. 4. You should pay a joining fee of $50.00. 5. You should be able to participate or at least attend all meetings held. 6. You should attend all the training lessons. 7. You should have no outstanding debts to the community e.g. you should have finished paying for the dam.
Duties of office bearers / leaders:	Chairperson: leads the meetings. Vice chairperson: assists the chairperson. Secretary: time keeper and writes minutes. Assistant Secretary: assists the secretary. Treasurer: keeps money. Committee members: help the heads / leaders. Leaders are chosen during the meeting by us the members of the group. They will lead for three years then elections for the new leaders will be held. If we feel we still need them on board they can be elected back to their seats.
Operational tasks / ways of working:	• There will be 3 teams for watering. • We will assist each other in watering our plants in case any one of our group member is not feeling well or in case of any emergency. • We will work together two (2) times a week on Tuesdays and Wednesdays. We aim to be at the gardens at 9 am and we will leave at 4 pm. • We will buy the seeds as a group. • Each member will be ploughing in their own beds.

(table continued on next page)

(Table 8.5 continued)	
Working relationships / rules:	1. If one has committed a crime, we will sit down and talk to them and they have to pay a fine of $100.00. If they fail to pay then s/he is no longer a member of our garden. 2. If one is resigning, s/he does not get anything because they will have just left. 3. If one does not come to meetings then s/he will pay a fine of $20.00 a day. 4. If one is late for meetings s/he has to bring a fine of $5.00. 5. If one is no longer coming for lessons, there is need for that person to get advice from others. If that does not work then that person is cancelled from the group. 6. If one steals from other members, that is if s/he is one of the members, we will sit down with them and talk to them, but if they continue then we are left with no choice but to chase them away from the group, but if one steals from the garden and is not from the group they are sent to court. 7. If one dies from the group, we talk to the family members. A new member can join from the family and continue from where the deceased left, if no one is willing to join then we continue by ourselves. 8. If one is not paying the membership fees as per agreement, we talk to that person and give them time to make that payment. If they fail to pay then we cancel them from the group. 9. If we are not using the garden as we are supposed to we will look for assistance from people like the Councillor and Chief.
How to handle money and its use (Banking):	There is a membership fee of $50.00 per person every month. In opening the book it will be signed by the chairperson, secretary, treasurer. Any two of the signatories will be the ones signing for the money at the bank. The money will be used in the case of: • Pump repairs – e.g., purchase of spare parts. • Any damage to the property in use – e.g., piping, taps or water tanks. • Buying seeds and pesticides. If it is less than $2,000.00 we keep it at home but if it is more than that we keep it at the bank (P.O.S.B).
How to handle our property:	Tanks: Should always be clean and also filled with water. Tools: We will appoint someone to be in charge of the tools. If we lose tools all members of the group should pay for them. We should only use the tools in our gardens. We should not take them for personal use and not lend them to anyone. Pumps: In case of any damage all members should assist each other in repairing the pumps. We will also give each other time to use the pumps. Gate: The gate will only be opened by the one chosen to keep the keys during working days.
Meetings:	A meeting of all members will be held on the last Wednesday of the month at 2 pm.
Signatures:	All members agree on what is written above.

Chapter summary

Human interactions and perceptions may well be the greatest limitation to the success of any water supply initiative. There is a plethora of technical information and qualified engineers that can usually be called on to design and implement a water supply scheme. Technically a scheme might be a hundred percent suitable, correctly designed, properly installed and fully operational, but unless there is a will by the vast majority to work together, the scheme will not become a sustainable asset of the community and will not provide those in need with the benefits of an improved water supply.

Agreement and harmony in the operation and management of a scheme is the most important factor and whether or not this is achieved will invariably determine the overall success of the project. There will always be some members of the community who are estranged for one reason or another and it is frequently with these people where problems arise. Every effort should be made, therefore, to bring those who have become alienated back into the community as without this their dissatisfaction may well pervade the entire community to the detriment of all.

If circumstances permit, capacity building and training will help by making people aware of problems and difficulties that other communities have faced in similar situations. All one can do is to make people aware of the challenges, both technical and social but at this stage people must resolve problems themselves. Ultimately, the operation and management of the water supply is something that communities must work out for themselves and the success or failure of a scheme will depend on the outcome.

9

Checklist for project suitability

IN THIS CHAPTER:
- Principles of effective abstraction systems
- A checklist and sequence of questions to consider for successful implementation of small-scale community sand-abstraction systems
- A flow chart of suitable site and abstraction technology
- Evaluation of sand-abstraction

SMAARTS checklist

Table 9.1 below represents a checklist of factors for consideration that are likely to ease and improve the abstraction of water from river sediment in an effective and sustainable manner.

- **Sustainability:** the technology must be such that end-users are able to understand and operate equipment for themselves and to supply their own solutions to keep it operational

- **Maintainability:** only basic procedures of installation, maintenance and repair should be used so that users are prepared to undertake maintenance work and to effectively respond to breakdowns

- **Acceptability:** a level of technology to which people are able to relate that ideally becomes a 'popular' technology where there is a sense of identity, ownership and responsibility

Table 9.1. SMAARTS test

A checklist of sociological and technological requirements for a successful adoption of sand-abstraction:	**S**ustainability **M**aintainability **A**cceptability **A**ffordability **R**eliability **T**ransferability **S**uitability

138

- **Affordability:** Pump parts should be affordable and available. Ideally fabricated from locally available or recycled materials which are unlikely to command great expense. Even better if the equipment itself can be locally fabricated

- **Reliability:** The equipment should be reliable and durable, ideally sturdy and consequently long-lasting

- **Transferability:** People should be able to associate with the technology, if necessary with appropriate technical training and sociological capacity building so that the technology can be successfully adopted in other localities. Ideally manufacture should be possible with only basic tools and without specialist equipment.

- **Suitability:** A suitable and effective technology with advantages which are clearly apparent in ease of abstraction, quantity or quality of water

Community checks

Identify a suitable community
The most successful water supply projects are those that are instigated by the beneficiaries. If the beneficiaries show little or no desire for a new, alternate water supply there will be little chance of a permanent, sustainable scheme.

Identify the users
Although it may not be possible to restrict the number of people who use the water supply, experience has shown that 15 to 20 users is an optimum number. The more the group has in common the greater their solidarity and the greater the likelihood of successful and sustainable use. A group with a common purpose such as a small irrigation project has the greatest chance of success.

Assess the leadership and likely capacity of the community
Solidarity understanding and agreement between users is all important. Any assistance that can be provided to help a group or community to work together successfully is time well spent.

Sand river and site selection

Identification of suitable sand rivers
A physical survey is required to determine whether or not the general conditions in the river valley are likely to be conducive for sand-abstraction development.

Identification of a site

A location must be identified on the river that gives the best chance of providing a permanent year-round water supply that is suitably sited for the convenience of users and water related projects. Chapter 3 provides additional information.

Identify a suitable abstraction system

A decision is required on which abstraction system and equipment is most suited to the site, the water yield and requirement, and the needs of the community. Relevant information is provided in Chapter 4.

Abstraction equipment – materials and equipment

Selection of a well-point or other abstraction system

Equipment selection is critical. The well-point must have a suitable size aperture in order to develop a natural screen within the sediment. The ingress of too much sediment will clog the well-point and abstraction pipes and create excessive wear on the pump parts.

Table 9.2 gives an indication of the likely performance of the common types of well-point, however with differing materials and several manufacturers

Well-point or caissons	Sustainability	Maintainability	Acceptability	Affordability	Reliability	Transferability	Suitability
Round aperture well-point	★★★	★★★★	★★★★★	★★★★	★★★★★	★★★★	★★★★
Longitudinal slot aperture well-point	★★★	★★★★	★★★★	★★★★	★★★★	★★★★	★★★
Transverse slot aperture well-point	★★★	★★★★	★★★	★★★★	★★★★	★★★★	★★
Synthetic textile covered well-point	★★★★	★★	★★★	★	★★★★	★	★★★
Infiltration gallery	★★★	★★★★	★★★	★	★★★★★	★	★★★★
No-fines concrete screen	★★★★	★★★★	★★★★	★★	★★★★	★	★★★

Table 9.2. SMAARTS ranking of well-points and no-fines concrete well-screens

Table 9.3. Appraisal of home made well-points and caissons

Type of well-point	Installation method	Suitability	Performance
uPVC pipe, round apertures	Driven or digging-in	Good – easily manufactured, adaptable, durable	Good
uPVC pipe, slot apertures	Driven or digging-in	Poor – prone to breakage during installation, likelihood of slots clogging with fines	Acceptable
Steel, round apertures	Driven or digging-in	Moderate – expensive materials, adaptable, durable	Good
No fines concrete sheath	Digging-in	Good – easy manufacture, adaptable, durable	Not suitable in all situations
Type of caisson			
Large diameter uPVC pipe, round apertures	Digging-in	Good – easy manufacture, adaptable, durable	Good
Two basins	Digging-in	Moderate – easy manufacture, adaptable	Not suitable in all situations

Photograph 9.1. Round aperture well-point

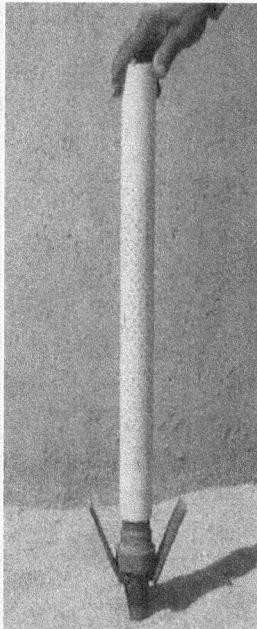

J. Hussey

141

of each type it cannot be considered definitive. Five stars score well, one star badly. The condition of the site also has considerable influence on the selection of the well-point or abstraction system.

Table 9.3 provides an appraisal of home-made well-points and small, uPVC and plastic caissons.

Of home-made well-points those with numerous round apertures have provided the best overall potential to date. Such well-points as shown in Photograph 9.1 (and also Figure 4.8) have shown that they can be used in a broad spectrum of conditions and are straightforward to fabricate and install.

Handpump selection

Pumps are of course critical to a successful sand-abstraction scheme and must be matched to the quantity and flow of water available, the height to which the water must be raised and the power source available.

Basic requirements of handpumps:

- Simplicity, easily understood design and operation
- Low-cost manufacture and assembly, minimal use of specialist tools or equipment
- Manufacture from readily available materials
- Ease of maintenance, readily procured materials for replacement parts, easily manufactured and easy fitment of parts with no specialist tools
- Reliability and durability
- User understanding and acceptability

Summary of suitable low-tech handpumps:

- *Displacement pump – bucket pump.* A suction pump with a single valve in the base and with a valve in the piston which water passes through on the down stroke.

  These pumps that include the basic Rower pump and Treadle pump are suitable in most sand-abstraction handpump applications direct coupled to well-points and can be fitted to caissons, sand wells, offset wells and infiltration gallery collector wells.

- *Displacement pump – force pump.* A suction pump with two valves, one foot valve and one side valve where water does not pass through the piston. Sometimes called a force pump as water is expelled from the pump cylinder by force.

These pumps that include the versions of the Rower pump, Treadle pump and the Dabane Trust Joma pump are suitable in most sand-abstraction handpump applications direct coupled to well-points and fitted to caissons, sand wells, offset wells and infiltration gallery collector wells.

- *Displacement pump – direct action pump.* Operates as a lift pump in water and is thus restricted to use in vertical well-points (tube-wells) in sand or gravelbeds, offset wells and infiltration gallery collector wells.
- *Direct lift – rope and washer pump.* A very simple and basic direct lift pump. The pump operates directly in water and due to the diameter of the driving wheel at the top has a width that generally restricts it to use on an offset well and infiltration gallery collector well. Excellent for simplicity but limited in its application.

Table 9.4 provides a simplified assessment of handpumps suitable for use on small-scale community based sand-abstraction schemes

Connecting pipes, suction and delivery piping

Identification of suitable pipe work, the design and diameter of the well-point and the connecting pipe must be determined by standard flow calculations that include the volume of water that will be carried, the velocity of the water through the pipe, the length of the pipe and the material used in the pipe. The nature of the site will also determine a suitable material for connecting pipes.

Steel piping is expensive and in time will rust, even galvanised piping is vulnerable to rust at the threads. Rigid uPVC pipe is cheaper but has little

Handpumps	Sustainability	Maintainability	Acceptability	Affordability	Reliability	Transferability	Suitability
Piston/suction lift pump	★★★★	★★★★	★★★★	★★★★	★★★	★★★★	★★★★★
Piston/suction force pump	★★★	★★★	★★★	★★★	★★★★	★★★	★★★★★
Direct action	★★★★	★★★★★★	★★★	★★★★★	★★	★★★★★	★★
Rope / washer	★★★★	★★★★★★	★★★	★★★★★	★★★★	★★★★	★★

Table 9.4. SMAARTS ranking of handpumps

flexibility and is liable to fracture if there is significant sediment transport through the river channel.

Low density polyethylene pipe (LDPE) is more expensive than rigid uPVC pipe but is easy to lay, has flexibility and in the appropriate grade or class can withstand atmospheric pressure.

Headworks

To determine a suitable water-point headwork consideration must be given to the source and yield of the water supply and whether or not there is a particular requirement for the water, domestic, livestock or food production use. It must be decided whether or not the water requires transfer, to a water standpoint, to a livestock water trough or to a garden. Further considerations are what designs are available and what materials are available for the construction of:

A clean domestic water supply

A secure bucket stand which prevents contaminated water from entering buckets and containers that are used to transport water should be incorporated into the design

Sump tanks

Water should flow easily into any sump tanks that are used for the onward passage of water, without fouling the pump surrounds

Livestock water troughs

Adequate fencing will be required to protect the pump from damage by cattle jostling for water

Water storage tanks

Particularly if the water is to be used for irrigation

Sanitation

Particularly when the water supply system is a component of a WATSAN based programme consideration should be given to:

Ensuring clean water is discharged into buckets and containers. A suitable delivery spout from the pump to the container will be required to ensure no contamination of water, no wastage of water and no pooling of water that will provide a breeding ground for mosquitoes.

The construction of washing sinks for clothes is a further possibility.

Toilets – very few toilets are provided with hand washing facilities, yet this is a fundamental requirement to reduce incidences of diarrhoea and the transfer of pathogens.

Hygiene – community toilets are often constructed at points such as business centres stores, gardens and schools but very few are equipped to meet the needs of women and girls in particular who periodically need discreet washing facilities.

Training

Appropriate training will better prepare communities and better ensure the sustainability of the equipment.

Considerations are:

Is there a functioning water-point management committee in place, what practical training and capacity building might be of assistance.

- What is the capability of the group or community in practical pump operation and maintenance
- What planning and practical skills does the community have
- What tools and materials are readily available within the community

Opportunities for sand-abstraction

Sand-abstraction together with other alternate sources is a water supply system that has very largely been overlooked by the established water supply industry. This is quite surprising when considering:

- The technology is based on borehole screen and pump equipment design. In the design of projects regular groundwater survey and design criteria are used
- The hydrogeology of sand-abstraction is also directly related to the groundwater and borehole industry
- It is a technology that is acceptable to end-users, based as it is on traditional water supply systems. This technology has up-graded traditional open unsafe sand well water supplies to sealed safe water supplies
- Preliminary assessments are easily carried out and installations can be effected by local artisans with a minimum of preparation or training
- Most of the materials and equipment for well-point and pump fabrication and for installation are generally available in industrially

developing countries. Fabrication procedures are not difficult and almost all components can be either sourced or fabricated locally

- In most situations sand-abstraction is a natural source of clean water
- With small-scale systems the technology is simple and basic to operate and manage, making it a sustainable source of water that most rural communities are able to operate and manage with minimal inputs
- There are instances of small-scale sand-abstraction systems in operation for at least 15 years managed entirely independently by groups of rural women. More than 100 successful small-scale schemes can be identified in western and southern Zimbabwe

Technology evaluation and appraisal

As with any water supply system it is well worth conducting a technical appraisal before engaging in the development of a sand-abstraction scheme and again on project completion. If undertaken correctly sand-abstraction technology has the potential to meet the objectives below.

Some of the questions are:

- Does it meet users expectations?
- Has it been a technology that users have accepted? Is it a simple, straightforward technology that has not required professional or high-tech geophysical surveys or specialist equipment to install or maintain?
- Is it a sustainable technology that people have been able to operate, maintain, repair and manage satisfactorily for themselves? Has the scheme required outside assistance to keep it going?
- Has it been cost-effective?
- Have the users been innovative and used the system and the water wisely? Have they been able to find solutions for themselves and if necessary to make adaptations?
- How transferable is the technology? To what degree might other communities who can obtain or adapt suitable materials and resources use these to set up their own schemes, and what degree of assistance might they require?

10

Case studies
and project evaluation

IN THIS CHAPTER:
- An account of four garden groups: their use, management systems and successes and failures

Case studies

A study of the success and failure of the systems used and the way users interact with both the technology and with themselves can provide learning examples for others and help to pin point any shortcomings in development or establishment methodologies. A review of the strategies and activities of community groups will help to identify what to look out for and points to note that can be passed on to others.

Background and common principles

The purpose and origins, the organizational structure and management system of the three groups is quite similar. However the achievements of the three groups differ considerably. Each group was supported by the Dabane Trust in Zimbabwe to make a start, each has a similar number of participants, a similar size garden and the same water abstraction system. Each is a ring fenced garden of a half to three quarters of a hectare in size with water drawn from a sand river by a dual handpump, Rower and Joma pump system. Water is initially drawn into a sump on the river bank by a Rower pump and from there again pumped by hand to a water storage tank in a garden from where it gravitates to some 9 dipping wells from which it can be quickly and easy applied to the nearby beds.

Each group has the same infrastructure and has received the same capacity building, record keeping and practical training. Each garden belongs to the group who worked together to make and erect the fence, to make bricks and then to work together with Dabane Trust staff to install the well-points and pumps, to build the pump headworks and the water storage tanks. The group members allocate land around each dipping well so that everyone has a similar distance to convey water. They work together in smaller teams to draw water and to keep the pumps operational. The beds however are individually managed and the income derived is the property of each member.

The three accounts have primarily been compiled from interviews with members of the group. Dialogue has been backed up with observation and analysis of reports that were made during the time the groups were being supported. The questions asked of each group were:

- What is the name of the group and where is it sited?
- When did the group form?
- Why did the group form?
- How did the group form?
- What is the number in the group?
- What is the management system used by the group?
- Which crops are grown and what is the production method?
- How is the crop and the income from the crop used?
- What were the problems faced and dealt with?
- What were the goals and expectations of the group?

The interviews were conducted with members of the three groups in July and August 2006 by food production and training programme unit leader Thelma Ntini of the Dabane Trust.

1. Toloki garden

The group has developed a high level of production in a well established fully independent garden where they grow 2 to 3 crops in a year. They particularly concentrate on brassica for which there is a very good local market from regular 'garden-gate' sales that can be supplemented with sales to a nearby hospital, a business centre and local schools. Group members also have dry-land arable fields but manage to keep the garden cropped throughout the year by growing in-season crops and a number of perennial crops.

The Toloki group has a garden near Tshelanyemba business centre, Ward 7 (Malaba), Matobo District, Matabeleland South. The group draws water

Photograph 10.1. Toloki garden

from the Shashane River a sand river more than 150 metres wide but only 1 to 2 metres deep due to underlying rock. There is however a permanent supply of water that the group uses throughout the year as required. The group is comprised of 10 women who came together in 1992 and have managed the garden ever since.

Crops grown are numerous. The group has been growing perennial kale for many years and much of the 1 hectare garden is cropped to this with some plants more than 2 metres high. The garden is also cropped with other brassica; thousand head kale, rape and choumollier but also onions, carrots and occasionally peas and beetroot. The group members have been selecting onion seed since the garden began and now grow onions almost as large as footballs! Tomatoes however do not do well as there has been a significant build up of red spider mite.

As the dry season progresses and the weather becomes too hot for vegetables the group generally has much of the garden planted to green mealies for which there is a ready local market. The crop is finished by Christmas by which time the group has planted sugar beans and pumpkins that only require a minimum of attention during the rains with some supplementary irrigation in poor rainfall years. The gardeners also grow chillies and have sugar cane and fruit trees such as paw paw, citrus and a small but heat tolerant apple.

When asked about their group and activities the members provided the following:

Our membership stands at 10. We are an all women's group. We started in 1992. Our garden draws water from the Shashane.

One of the founder members left the area in 1999 to live in Bulawayo. Her place was taken over by another lady from the same village.

Our aim is to grow vegetables for family consumption and to sell the surplus to our neighbours. We grow different kinds of vegetables such as rape, choumollier, cabbage, spinach, tomatoes and onions. The onions that we grow we use the seed that we produce ourselves and we have been using this seed since 1993. We also grow maize in summer and each member owns two fruit trees. These range from oranges, pawpaws, lemons, peaches, guavas to uxakuxaku and umnyi.

We have been trained in basic gardening skills and food preservation. We have never had the opportunity to dry the vegetables because all the vegetables are sold fresh.

We have a constitution that we try to follow but we have relaxed some of the bye-laws that we set. We no longer buy seed as a group, each individual sources their own seed but we do agree on which crops to grow where. With the income from the garden some of us have bought goats, sheep, chickens, wheelbarrows, hoes, pots, dishes and food during drought years. Some have been able to pay school fees for their children who are at school. We have not started any project from the proceeds from the vegetables as a group but one of the members managed to acquire a grinding mill, part of the money was income from the garden.

Photograph 10.1 shows the perennial nature of Toloki garden with fruit trees, perennial kale and chillies. The picture also shows selected onions left for seed. In the background is the Shashane sand river.

2. Sizanani garden

The gardeners are a group, in their own words, committed to improving the food security status of their families. They operate the irrigated garden in conjunction with dry-land crop farming; using the garden as and when they wish. In seasons when dry-land crops have failed there is a very high level of production, but there is little or no use made of the garden when there has been better rainfall and the members have secured a reasonable dry-land harvest.

The Sizanani group operates a garden in Silonkwe village, administrative ward 12 (Sontala), Matobo District, Matabeleland South. It is a food security group that manages a small-scale irrigated garden during the dry-

Photograph 10.2. Sizanani garden

season winter months, integrated with rain fed dry-land arable farming in the summer. They use the garden as and when they wish, producing a large quantity of crops when dry-land crops fail and make little or no use of the garden when there is a reasonable dry-land harvest. The garden is a ring-fenced enclosure of half a hectare that is watered by handpumps that draw water from the Sansukwe sand river through a collector well.

The garden group formed in 1996 with the intention of providing additional and more nutritious food for their families and supplementing the staple food diet of the local community. A particular concern was to ensure an adequate supply of food all year round, particularly in the dry-season when fresh nutritious food was in short supply. A further reason was to generate a financial income.

The origin of the group was in a savings club that was formed to assist the members to purchase basic kitchen utensils. Through an interview on the radio the group learned of the Dabane Trust programmes and decided to approach the organization for assistance to start a group garden. Each savings club member already had a traditional garden but invariably the brushwood fencing did not prevent cattle and goats from breaking into garden and destroying the vegetables.

The group is comprised of 14 members, 13 women and 1 man. The number has been 14 throughout but was initially 12 women and 2 men. When one of the men grew old and could no longer manage the work he ceded his vegetable beds to his daughter-in-law so that they would remain with his family.

The group has a dual system of management of the garden, they work together when there is a common need on such things as maintaining the fence and repairing the pump. Teams of 5 work together on pumping duty to fill the water storage tank and to water their vegetable beds. The beds are individually managed with production and sales accruing to the individual member. Typically family members assist the group by digging through, cultivating and watering beds.

Vegetables grown are choumollier and rape, carrots, onions and tomatoes as well as maize and beans. The crops grown depend on the season and customer demand. Much of each crop is consumed by the members' family and the rest is sold to neighbours. The gardeners are able to establish a very good trade in tomatoes and their kale production is legendary, green and succulent, it is so successful in fact that they are able to sell 'futures'. In order to secure a supply of kale, vendors often make payment on a crop as soon as it is established after transplanting.

Income is typically used to pay schools fees, to meet regular monthly expenditure and general family needs. Some members have purchased items such as wheelbarrows, blankets, three-legged cooking pots, blankets and household appliances.

Unfortunately the water source is not always reliable and is liable to dry up in drought years. The group reports that if this was not the case they would be able to grow crops year round, however the reality is that even in a good season the garden is not worked year round and at the onset of the rains the members always stop irrigated garden activities in favour of dryland crop farming.

The group states that they would like to "generate sufficient funds to purchase 2 heifers and start a 'pass-on-the-calf' scheme so that the 14 of us can own our very own cow". They also reported that they have hosted some groups who came for exchange visits. The chairlady said, "We hope visiting us has improved their cohesion and production. We are a united group and we plan the garden activities together. The meetings that we have had also improve our relationships as villagers". They also take pride in what they say was a wonderful commissioning of the garden which coincided with Dabane's 10 year celebration of involvement in rural development work in 2001.

Photograph 10.2 shows the high level of production that the gardeners of Sizanani garden are able to achieve.

3. Khulumsenza garden

The Khulumsenza garden group was a pioneer garden group in a traditional livestock area where sorghum and millet crops are more typical than maize and fresh vegetables were unknown. The garden draws its water from the Manzamnyama River which drains into the Makgadikagdi Pan in central Botswana where it is lost to evaporation. Although essentially a livestock area it is a depressed area with many men working in urban centres in Botswana or South Africa. Many of these migrants return home once a year at Christmas and only remit money home infrequently at other times. Consequently many women are left to manage the family and the home alone and unaided and find the provision of adequate nutritious food a particular problem.

The group has a garden in Ndutshwa village 1, ward 8 (Huwana). Bulilima District, Matabeleland South. The group was formed in 1995 so that the members could produce food for their families and meet a market opportunity as there was no regular supply of vegetables within some 80 kilometres of Ndutshwa and even that centre was dependent on a production and retail centre at a further 100 kilometres.

The headmaster of the local primary school had worked with Dabane Trust in the Gwanda area. When he was transferred to Huwana primary school he told the community there of the sand-abstraction work the Trust was developing. An invitation was sent to Dabane and as a result four garden groups were assisted along the river.

Photograph 10.3. Khulumsenza garden

The Khulumsenza group was initially comprised of 30 members, all women. However only 13 still remain, 8 from the original group with 5 members who joined more recently. The members who have been with the group since its inception are now aging, consequently they are dependent on younger members of their family to undertake any heavy physical work, which basically amounts to all work other than watering. The group adopted the approach of working together to manage the garden but each member cropped their own vegetable beds. The garden was cropped sporadically, some years it was well managed and other years not so well.

At its peak many types of vegetables were grown, perennial kale was a favourite as were tomatoes, which were particularly lucrative. Crops such as carrots, onions and beans were popular and the group also grew green peas which had never been seen in the area before. Crops such as choumollier, rape and green maize were grown regularly depending on the season and a lot of vegetables were sold. Quantities of livestock manure were applied to the beds and adequate mulching was carried out.

Each family received sufficient vegetables for relish and was able to supplement diets during seasons of inadequate rainfall by growing crops such as sugar beans and green mealies. In addition sufficient money was generated for school fees and the purchase of school books and uniforms. Several members of the group banded together and by pooling their income were able to pay medical fees and to establish a burial fund.

On the whole the group did work together well for several years. They overcame any operational problems together, at times a guard was employed to keep marauding monkeys out of the garden and to protect the water-point from elephants. Sufficient use was made of the garden, a pit latrine was constructed and the gardeners maintained the pumps and the water tanks adequately.

Overall it was a productive group, generally considered successful – until some members stopped filling the water tank after they had watered and the team coming the next day found an empty tank. The group was unable to resolve the problem, the situation worsened and the garden fell into disuse for two years. No maintenance was carried out, white ants destroyed the fence posts and the fence collapsed. Following a particularly poor rainy season some members restarted the garden, the pumps were brought into use and the garden was cropped again. However the group had been demoralized and were not prepared to work together. The fence was not repaired, even though the netting was still on the ground around the garden. Consequently when the garden was in maximum production, with the fence down some rogue cattle walked in one night and decimated the garden .

Photograph 10.3 shows the crops that were grown in the Khulumsenza garden before the group experienced difficulties in their working relationships.

Comments from the group:

- Whilst we met as a group we used to relate to each other as villagers this enhanced our relationship

- We started grocery clubs and burial clubs because a number of the group members (five) have died due to HIV/AIDS related illnesses

- Spare parts are a problem. The pumps are not working well, they are worn out

- We are thinking of cutting down the size of the garden

- The fence is not strong, livestock break in and destroy the crops. The water dries up during droughts. Last year we did not grow any crops because it was a very bad year. We have decided that we are going to decrease the size of the garden so that we can strengthen the fence. The garden was meant for 30 people, it is just too big

- The main water storage tank is now leaking. We have not repaired the facilities. It was our fault, we left the tanks without water for a long time.

4. Legion Mine garden

This garden was also one of the early gardens established with the assistance of Dabane Trust. Unfortunately in spite of considerable effort on the part of Dabane Trust training staff it has not been possible to interview the group.

The garden started in 1993 and was extremely productive with one member in particular working exceptionally hard and very well organized. He produced volumes of vegetables with his family, beyond the needs of the local community. As a result he made a contract with a nearby mission hospital and used his donkey cart to transport vegetables there and to the local stores and business centre as well clinics and schools and the local police station in the area. Almost everyday he had a load of vegetables for sale that he was transporting up to 20 kilometres.

Unfortunately this person was not liked within the community or by the rest of the group who accused him of taking an unfair advantage. Squabbles broke out that no one could resolve. Before long the group broke up and since 1995 the garden has not been used.

Project evaluation and appraisal

No system or project can be considered complete without adequate monitoring and evaluation. It is important to consider the following criteria and to establish whether or not the final project can be considered successful. There are technical considerations to review and several socio-cultural issues, several of which can be related to the case study examples above. There is no right or wrong answer and no standard solution.

It is important to seek ways to ensure the sustainability of community water supplies and an important first step is to keep an open mind and to regularly analyse situations and information. The following are specific points that should be considered and the results will vary with each project evaluated:

- Has sand-abstraction worked – has a correct and effective water supply system been put in place
- Are the users in control of the scheme and generally satisfied with it
- Is the system sustainable – what has been the maintenance/repair and downtime
- Is the community getting the water that was initially assessed and is the scheme providing all the water for which it was planned and designed. Have there been significant losses of water at any point
- What have been the greatest obstacles for the community or group to deal with and overcome
- What use has the community made of the water – was this as planned
- What has been the eventual quality of the water after it has been abstracted
- How can the project management be assessed. Has the community worked together and made the best use of the water supply or has the project been beset with acrimony and consequently has been under utilized.

A1

Technical selection, design and construction process

IN THIS APPENDIX:
- Design criteria – equipment required
- Technical solutions – description and calculations to determine and design a small-scale sand-abstraction system
- Construction of pump headworks

Design criteria

The correct design of abstraction equipment is critical to a successful installation. Equally important is identification of the right equipment for a proposed site and if necessary modification of the technology or the physical conditions of the site.

To establish a satisfactory and successful sand-abstraction scheme each part of the system requires careful design and preparation, with each component matched. The overall abstraction system and pump layout will be determined by several factors:

- the anticipated yield of the water supply
- the available power
- the height of a suitable site above the water-level
- the height of the water discharge point above the pump site.

Each factor must be matched to the conditions and to each component:

- The screen area of the abstraction system should be suitable for the sediment surrounding it, the volume of water and the pump
- The pump must be appropriate for the abstraction system and the site

- The site must be safe and convenient for users and either suitable or adapted to the pump, the point of water discharge and the source of power
- The power that is available must be appropriate to the abstraction system, the pump and the site.

Each component must be designed or altered and adapted as necessary to make each compatible with another. Well-screens can be designed for the sediment and the yield of the pump. The pump can be designed for the yield of the water supply, the power available and the site. And the pump site can be raised or lowered to best advantage in relation to the water source and the discharge point.

Small-scale systems, particularly those in dry-land areas require careful design so that the systems that are put in place are compatible one with another.

The yield of the pump should not exceed the water supply or the energy available or the design capacity of the well-point.

The quantity of water and the height to which it is to be pumped should not exceed the power available – which with small-scale systems is frequently human power and very often female, and then either very young or elderly.

In order to achieve a satisfactory installation it is most appropriate to plan the design of a water supply system commencing from the aspect over which there is least control. In many areas where sustainable, small-scale, community supply schemes are required there are old and infirm people, some of whom can be expected to be sick and weak, possibly HIV positive, but who will still be required to pump and carry water. Thus the water supply must not exceed the available energy of the community nor the source of water that is available.

Small-scale systems, particularly those in dry-land areas require careful design so that the systems that are put in place are compatible one with another.

The yield of the pump should not exceed the water supply or the energy available or the design capacity of the well-point.

The quantity of water and the height to which it is to be pumped should not exceed the power available – which with small-scale systems is frequently human power and very often female, and then either very young or elderly.

The handpump should be designed so that two people may pump together if necessary. If there is an adequate supply of water, provided it does not become over abstracted, it is more appropriate to install a second or even a third small pump system than it is to install one larger pump for which there is no suitable source of power.

In reality the starting point of a small-scale water supply system is identification of the most significant limiting factor, whether this is the yield of water, the available power or depths from, or heights to which water must be pumped. From this a correlation can be made with other components of the scheme.

Power requirements

The available power is often the limiting factor of a small-scale handpump water supply. Although a strong, healthy person is able to develop up to 1kW of power for a few minutes, only some 0.2 – 0.25kW can be developed for any period of time. A high power output cannot be maintained as muscles in the human body easily become tired. If the person is aged or lacking in health their power output will be considerably reduced, or more likely, they will use the pump for a shorter period of time.

To achieve the greatest effectiveness a pump must be as efficient as possible, thus seals and valves must be maintained and the power available maximized. One method of improving the power output of the human body is to use the larger muscles in the back or legs, together with the weight of the body when pumping – rather than just the muscles of the arms.

A handpump with an average yield of 1.00 to 2.00m³/hr is a reasonable choice for one average to strong person or for two frail to average people to use together as a community pump water supply.

Pump requirements

An efficient pump that is in good working condition is required to optimize the quantity of water pumped and to ensure that energy, particularly human energy is not wasted. Handpumps such as the Rower pump which use back muscles and upper body weight and the Treadle pump which uses the large muscles of the leg and full body weight are both suitable pumps for small-scale sand-abstraction. Counterbalances that even out the energy required on each pump stroke also provide an advantage when pumping. A counterbalance can make pumping easier on both a direct reciprocating action pump and a rotary action pump.

Designed for use on shallow tube-wells the Rower pump has been proven to be a very suitable pump for small-scale sand-abstraction use. The pump is called a rower pump as to use it requires the action of rowing a boat. This requires operating the pump from a sitting position and leaning back on the draw stroke so that the weight of the upper body and not just the arm muscles is used to raise water. With this action some people are able to pump continuously for more than 30 minutes at a time. Other advantages of the Rower pump are the minimal materials that are required and the very simple construction that helps to make it a community-sustainable pump.

The 2 inch (50mm I.D.) SWS Rower pump has been designed to deliver water at up to 1l/sec (3.6m³/hr) and with two strong people pumping has yielded more than this. With the power generally available under practical, sustained pumping conditions the pump draws water from depths of up to 5.00m at 1 to 2m³/hr.

Performance data provided for a Bangladesh Rower pump with a 63mm cylinder (2½" pump) from trials conducted for the World Bank by the Consumer Association in the U.K.:

- Pumping head: 7.0 metres
- Pumping rate: 15 cycles per minute
- Volume: 27 litres per minute, (1.6m³/hr)
- Input: 48 watts
- Efficiency: 64%
- Maximum handle force: 20 kgf
- Volume discharged per stroke about 1.8 litres.

Comments provided by Richard Cansdale from his experience with the SWS Rower pump which he designed:

- The 2 inch pump is recommended to a maximum depth of 6.0 metres and the 2 ½ inch pump to a maximum of 4.5 metres.
- Flow from both pumps averages 1.0l/sec. There is a greater yield per stroke from the larger diameter pump, but this requires greater effort so in terms of work it evens out.

Pump site requirements

An ideal site for a pump is within 5 metres of the lowest level to which water will drop in the sediment of the river channel. This point will ideally be above the maximum flood level of the river. If this is not possible the pump site will require protection so that it is not unduly damaged during flood events.

The pump site should also be within some 10 metres of the highest point of water discharge – generally the top of the inlet pipe of a water tank. If this is not possible a second, booster pump installation should be installed. Although more effort is required with this triple pump system it has been shown that it is possible to raise water to an overall height of over 25 metres.

A pump site should also have easy access and importantly not be the cause of any erosion or environmental degradation. All digging, foundations and trenches must be adequately back-filled and not become water collection points. The installation must not be the cause of any water movement that will create runnels that will eventually lead to erosion of soil. Adequate fencing to protect equipment from damage or fouling by livestock or other animals should also be encouraged. In their search for water, elephants in some areas in Zimbabwe can sometimes be a significant cause of damage to pumps.

Small-scale sand-abstraction systems

Chapters 3, 4, 5 and 6 indicate the broad situations in which sand-abstraction is a suitable technology choice. Information is also provided on the wide range of sand-abstraction and pump equipment that is available and methods of selecting a suitable water abstraction system. With the technology and information available it is possible to identify the correct abstraction system within given conditions.

Although not appropriate in all situations a well-point system that is driven into river channel sediment and connected to a suction pump on the riverbank generally provides a simple, satisfactory and low-cost solution for a small-scale clean water supply. As such, an explanation and design of a typical single well-point sand-abstraction system is provided.

A simple small-scale single well-point system

The Dabane Trust has installed simple handpump technology sand-abstraction systems at more than 100 sites in Zimbabwe over a period of 15 years. The original installations put in place in 1992 are still in operation, independently managed by rural community groups.

Figure A1.1 shows the layout of a typical small-scale sand-abstraction system as developed by Dabane Trust with a single home-made well-point and a flexible connecting pipe to a rower pump on the riverbank. The rower pump is situated no more than 5 metres above the saturated river sediment level and discharges water into a sump. Water is then transferred a greater distance and height by a Joma pump to a water supply point such as a water storage tank in a garden. This can be several hundred metres distant and some 8 metres higher. The Joma pump uses rower pump components in uPVC pipe work with standard pipe fittings mounted in a steel frame. A treadle pump would provide an alternative to the Joma pump.

The following is a description of general sand-abstraction requirements with examples of the systems and design calculations for the equipment typically used by Dabane Trust.

Well-point requirements

As has been dealt with in preceding chapters a suitable well-point or infiltration gallery is required for the sediment conditions at a proposed site. The screen must have an aperture size, a diameter and a length that is suitable for the output of the pump and the grade of sediment in the river channel.

A number of commercial screens are available which have mainly been derived from the borehole screen industry. A list of some manufactures that make screens suitable for sand-abstraction use is contained in Appendix 2.

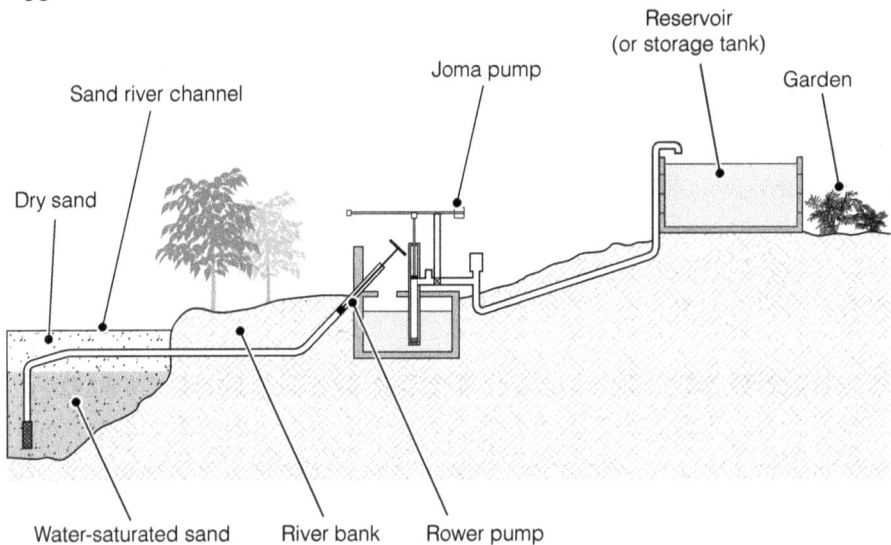

Figure A1.1. Layout of simple well-point sand-abstraction system

Calculation of screen aperture size

Correct screen aperture size is best ascertained by sieving. The ideal is to obtain an accurate grading of a sample of sediment. There are commercial companies that will carry out a sieve analysis and the Engineering Department of a University or a laboratory that analyses building materials or concrete mixtures may have a set of sieves that will provide a sediment analysis.

If such sophisticated equipment is not available approximations for gauging sediment particle size should be made as indicated in Chapter 3.

The size of apertures of a screen should ideally allow no more than 75% of the sediment to pass through, although in reality 85 or 90% may have to be acceptable. As explained in chapter 4 this will allow a natural screen pack to develop around the well-point without causing either undue wear on the moving parts of the pump or allowing the abstraction and pump system to clog up with sediment.

Thus if 10 - 25% of a sediment sample is retained on a 3.0mm sieve a screen with a 3.0mm aperture is suitable, but if less than 10% is retained then a smaller diameter aperture will be required. An assessment of the quantity of sediment that has been retained in a stack of sieves with decreasing apertures will help to determine screen slot size.

Local manufacture of a well-point screen is quite feasible. Round apertures can be formed by drilling or by pushing a red-hot wire through a uPVC pipe. These are generally clean sided, unlike slots cut with a hacksaw that tend to retain uPVC particles or kerf where the sawblade breaks through and which is relatively difficult to remove. Screens that have been formed by slots (2.35mm width) cut with a hacksaw blade in a uPVC pipe tends to fracture between the slots even if off-set, when the well-point is driven into sediment.

Realistically it is not feasible to drill holes smaller than 2.0mm. If a size smaller than this is indicated an alternative such as a screen with large apertures that is wrapped in geotextile, or a commercially available screen, such as a Boode ceramic screen will be required.

Calculation of the number and position of apertures

Having established the size of the aperture a calculation is required to determine the number of apertures that will ensure a low velocity of flow through alluvium to the screen. Not only the number but the position of each aperture is important as there must be sufficient material retained between each hole so that the screen is not unduly weakened. A further consideration in the calculation is the length of the screen which should not be too long. During periods of low water in the sediment the water-level should not drop below the level of the upper apertures which would allow air to be drawn into the system and lead to pump failure.

Well-point design

Step 1 – Pump yield

Determine an appropriate pump yield for the water source. A suitable output for a handpump is 1 to 2m³/hr. Depending on the permeability of the sediment 1 to 2m³/hr is also a sustainable yield for a single well-point. For yields larger than this multiple well-point systems are required.

Step 2 – Diameter and wall thickness of a well-point screen

Determine the inside diameter of the pipe to be used as a well-point. Suppliers and/or technical brochures should have information on the outside diameter and the wall thickness. A suitable pipe is a 50mm uPVC pipe. uPVC is measured by its outside diameter (O.D.) and thus irrespective of the class, (the wall thickness), will always be of the same diameter. A 50mm uPVC pipe will fit within a 50mm (2 inch) steel water pipe, (often referred to as a 2 inch, or 50mm galvanized steel water pipe), as the internal diameter of a 2 inch steel pipe is nominal and closer to 2.125 inches than 2 inches. The O.D. of the uPVC pipe is 50mm and the steel pipe has a nominal bore of 54mm.

Step 3 – Diameter of apertures

Calculate the aperture size from a sample of sediment – as above

NOTE: In order to avoid any confusion when joining uPVC pipe to steel water pipe it should be noted that because uPVC pipe is classified by its outside diameter and steel pipe by its inside diameter the same size uPVC and steel pipes do not join together without adaptors.

A uPVC pipe always joins to a smaller size steel pipe.

Thus for example a 63mm uPVC pipe couples with a 50mm (2 inch) steel pipe, which depending on the class and thus the I.D of the uPVC pipe, may create a restricted flow.

Step 4 – Internal velocity
Decide the velocity of flow through the internal diameter (I.D.) of the well-point pipe. A recommended flow is 0.03m/sec.

Step 5 – Material between the apertures
Determine a suitable distance between the sides of each aperture to maintain sufficient strength in the pipe. This will depend on the size of the apertures, large diameter apertures require a greater space between them than smaller apertures. As a useful guide the width of the material between the apertures should be twice the diameter of the aperture.

Step 6 – Number of apertures around the pipe
Calculate the number of apertures around the pipe at the distance decided in step 5. Adjust the distance to an even measurement between each aperture and rounddown.

D = pipe circumference/(aperture diameter + distance between apertures)

$$D = rounddown\big((\pi * d_p)/(d_a + L_a)\big)$$

Step 7 – Total number of apertures in the screen
Calculate the number of apertures to be made that will achieve the same velocity of flow through the screen, as through the well-point pipe.

Na = ((yield in m³/s)/velocity)/(area of aperture)

$$N_a = \left(\frac{Y}{3600 * v}\right) / \left(\frac{\pi * d^2}{4}\right)$$

Particularly in screens with a large number of small diameter apertures this could be increased by a nominal 10% to compensate for the friction created in the flow of water against the side of the apertures. However this would also lead to an increase in the overall length of the screen, which might then make the screen too long to be practical.

Step 8 – Number of rows of apertures
Calculate the number of holes required along the pipe at the same distance as determined in step 6. If possible increase by about 25% to compensate for apertures that are likely to block during the life of the screen. Check that the final screen is not an unreasonable length for the depth of sediment at the site. A rough guide is 10 to 20% of the depth of sediment.

Number of rows (Nr) = Na/D

Adjustment = Nd

Actual number of rows M = Nr + Nd

Actual number of apertures N= D*M

$$N = D * \left(\frac{N_a}{D} + N_d \right)$$

Step 9 – Check calculation for overall suitability

From the number of apertures finally decided on, recalculate the velocity of water through the screen to ensure that this has not become significantly greater than that determined in step 4.

Velocity = (yield in m³/s)/(Num apertures * area of aperture)

$$v_1 = \left(\frac{Y}{3600} \right) / \left(N_a * \frac{\pi * d^2}{4} \right)$$

From this data a well-point can be fabricated or purchased that will have suitable size apertures and will ensure the water abstracted from the sediment is at a velocity that will not cause any breakdown or deterioration in the equipment. Photograph A1.1 shows the aperture arrangement of a driven well-point and the use of a simple jig to achieve the correct distribution of apertures where several well-points are required. The diameter of the drill and the number of apertures drilled are determined in steps 3 to 9 above.

Well-point installation

A well-point or a number of well-points linked together must be installed as deep as possible at a suitable site in the river. The well-point as designed above can be made from a length of steel water pipe or from uPVC pipe closed at one end. Such a well-point can be dug into the sediment late in the dry season when the water-level in the river sediment is low. Alternatively a steel pipe can be driven into the river sand with a heavy hammer, however care must be taken not to damage any exposed threads on the well-point.

A suitable well-point can be made from uPVC pipe and equipped with a steel tip. This well-point can then be driven to the base of the river channel

Example:

Step 1, required yield: 1.5m³/hr

Step 2, internal diameter of the well-point: selected pipe 50mm O.D. uPVC pipe with 3.00mm wall thickness – internal diameter 44mm

Step 3, diameter of well-point apertures: from a sieve analysis of sediment at the installation site – 3.00mm

Step 4, internal velocity within the well-point: 0.03m/sec is recommended

Step 5, determine the distance between apertures on the circumference of the well-point (twice the diameter of the aperture) – 6.00mm

Step 6, calculate the number of apertures around the well-point, using the formula – 17

Step 7, determine the number of apertures required for the above statistics, using the formula – 1,965

Step 8, calculate the number of rows of apertures required, using the formula – 116.

Increase the number of rows by 10 to 25% to accommodate blockages – 128 (10%)

Adjust the number of apertures, using the formula – 2,169

Step 9, recalculate the velocity through the screen, as a check, using the formula – 0.0272m/sec

Allowing for a 25% blockage of the screen from lodged grains of sediment and incrustation of salts the velocity will be increased to 0.036m/sec, which is still quite adequate.

From other calculations of this example:

Length of screen – 796mm

Surface area of the screen – 12.3%

Photograph A1.1. Use of a jig in the construction of well-points

using a removable steel driving tube and a heavy hammer, which does not come into contact with the uPVC well-point.

An appropriate well-point fabricated from uPVC pipe with a sacrificial steel point to make a driven well-point is shown in Figure A1.2.

Handpump requirements

Direct action suction pumps are suitable handpumps for small-scale sand-abstraction use. A simple and effective pump that has been used successfully by Dabane Trust that is basic in both design and operation and is thus highly suitable for remote area use is the Rower pump. The Rower is a simple open-ended displacement pump which uses standard components and although the pump is available commercially it can also be manufactured locally.

Handpump components

The basic components of a Rower pump with a straightforward connection to a well-point include an inlet pipe, a foot valve, piston and piston rod. The following is a description of the purpose of the components together with the materials from which they can be made:

Inlet pipe – Purpose, a pipe through which water is drawn from a well-point, or from a well to a pump.

Accurate calculations are required to determine the size and class of the pipes that will connect the well-point(s) to a handpump. However, suitable materials for a small-scale single well-point/handpump installation as described above are likely to be 40mm LDPE (Low Density Polyethylene)

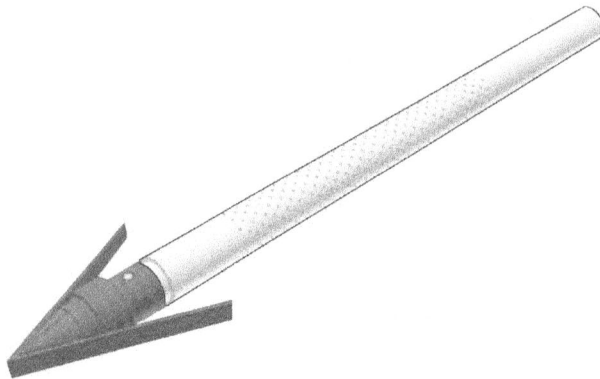

Figure A1.2. Round aperture well-point

which will pass through the river sediment and connect to a 50mm uPVC class 10 pipe on the riverbank, which in turn will connect to the handpump. Larger installations will require larger piping and fittings.

Foot valve – Purpose, a check valve in the bottom of the pump to allow water to enter the pump cylinder but not to flow back.

In the systems described foot valves are only located in the pumps. There is no foot valve located in the well-point or the connecting pipe where a grain of sediment lodged under the flap valve might render the system unusable. Suitable materials for simple valves are – uPVC sheet of 10 or 12mm thickness or discs of flattened uPVC pipe built up to 10 or 12mm; rubber flap from a light vehicle inner tube held in place with a 4,00mm × 20mm self-tapping stainless steel domed screw. The uPVC disc is cut to fit inside the pump cylinder and is drilled with 8 holes, 4×6mm and 4×8mm which are clear of the edges of the disc and of the centre. The rubber flap is fitted to the centre of the disc and held in place with the self tapping screw.

Pump cylinder – Purpose, a pipe or cylinder in the base of which the foot valve fits and through which the piston moves up and down.

Suitable materials for the system described - 63mm class 16 uPVC pipe

Piston – Purpose, moving check valve within the pump cylinder. It allows water which is held by the foot valve to flow through it as it is pushed downward and lifts water as it is pulled up.

There must be an airtight seal between the piston body and the cylinder so that air can be evacuated from the system in order for the pump to draw water. Suitable materials for fabrication of a piston are – layers of 10 or 12mm uPVC sheet or flattened uPVC pipe built up to a total thickness of 30mm, a rubber valve flap, rubber cup seals. Similar to the fixed foot valve the piston is also drilled with 4×6mm and 4×8mm holes.

Piston rod – Purpose, a shaft and tee bar which raises and lowers the piston within the pump cylinder. The rod passes through the centre of the piston and holds the rubber valve in place on top of the piston.

Suitable materials – 10mm bright steel rod, 2×10mm hex nuts, 1×10mm nyloc nut, 20mm black steel pipe.

A sketch of a Rower pump foot valve and piston fabricated from the materials listed above is shown in Figure A1.3.

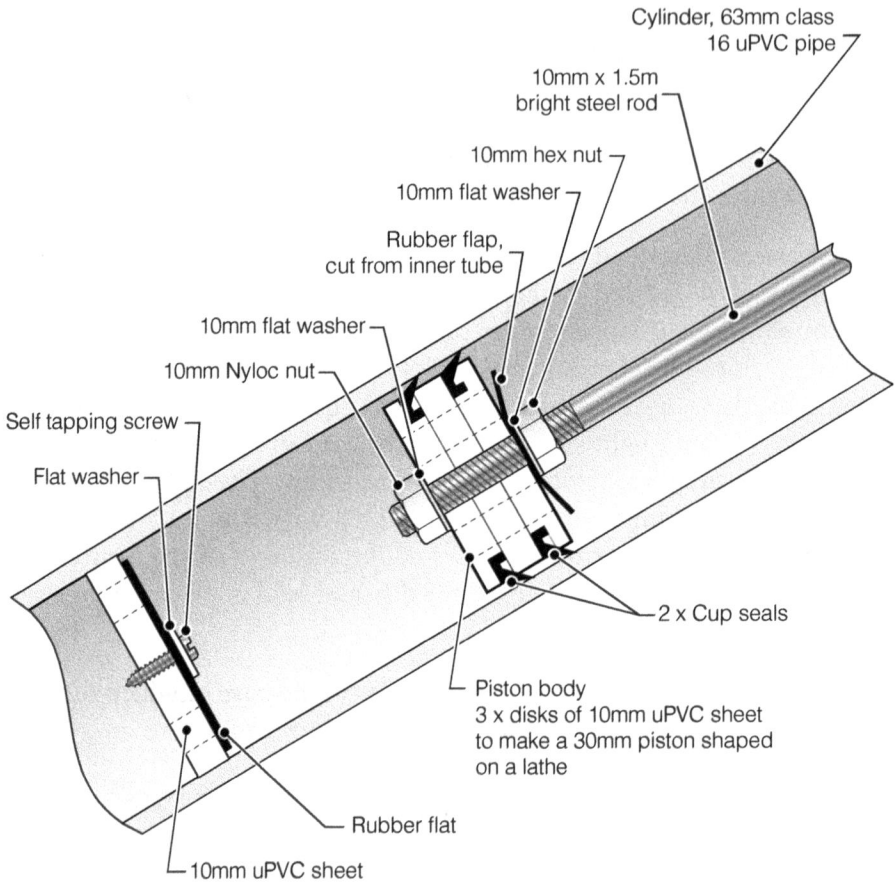

Figure A1.3. Components of a Rower pump

Pump and well-point installation calculations

The height from the water-level to the pump site must be calculated. At sea level where there is maximum atmospheric pressure this could theoretically be as much as 9.8 metres, however the actual lift will be determined by the efficiency of the pump to create a vacuum and will reduce by some 300mm for every 1,000 metres of altitude. In reality a lift of some 4 to 5 metres at an altitude of ±1,500 metres is quite acceptable. Consideration must also be given to the weight of water raised. Although it would be quite possible to construct a pump with an internal cylinder diameter of 63 or 75mm to raise a large volume of water over say 5 metres, the operation of the pump would most likely be beyond the capability of most handpump users.

Construction of pump head works

Head works for the pump system must be fully suited to the proposed use of the water. However as the intended purpose may change and as invariably it is clean, safe water that is drawn from river alluvium a general purpose style head work that enables easy collection of water for household use is probably best considered from the outset.

Photograph A1.2 shows a livestock drinking trough beside the Manzam-nyama River, Bulilima District, Matabeleland South, Zimbabwe. The trough is filled by a Rower pump that is direct coupled to a well-point. At one end of the trough and directly under the pump is a bucket stand for immediate collection of water before any contamination can occur. If there is no bucket in place water flows directly into the trough. The scheme is community owned and managed. The pump operators are protected from the cattle by a stout fence and in order to further safeguard the infrastructure from possible damage by pushing cattle the owners are always in attendance when the cattle are drinking. In the base of each trough a connection is fitted for a pump to draw water a further distance to a small irrigated garden.

Photograph A1.2. Makhulela community sand-abstraction water supply

Sloping bucket stand
to allow water to drain
into the drinking trough

Rower pump fitted
into wall for support

Livestock drinking trough

Directive spout to reduce
contamination of water

Protective wall for
pump and
connecting pipe

Connecting pipe from well point in sand
installed in a protective wall at 30° from
the horizontal for convenient operation
of the pump operator

Pump operators seat

An outlet may be installed in the
base of the trough for connection
to a garden water tank

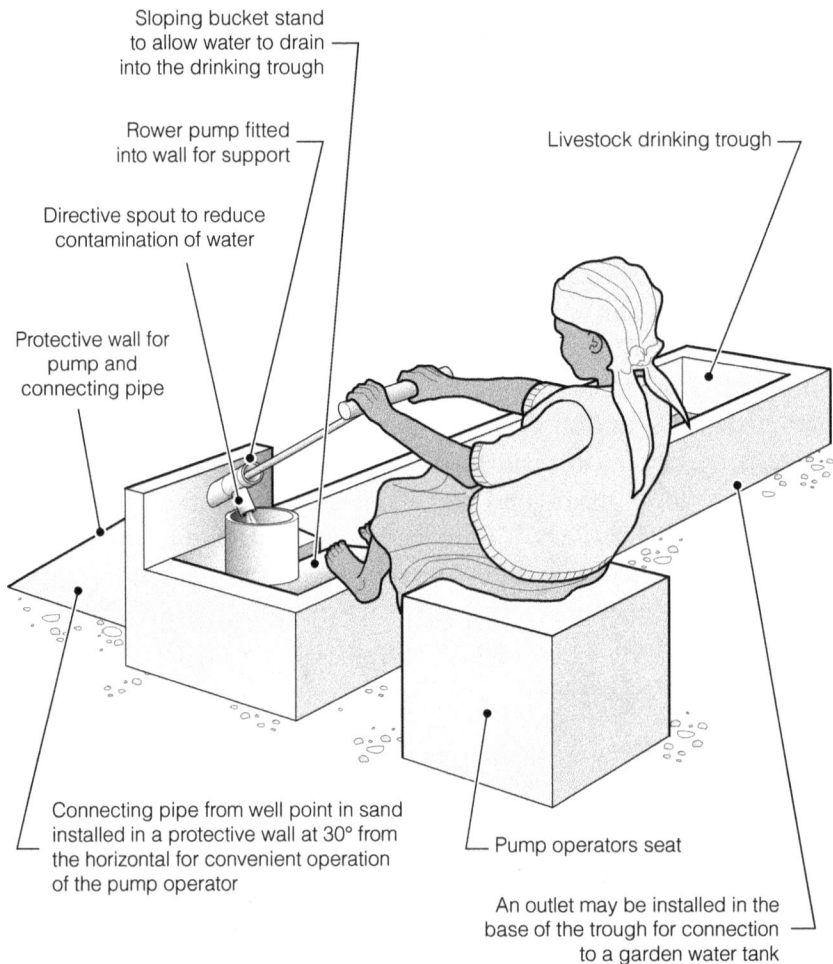

Figure A1.4. Household water supply point with livestock
drinking trough

The design of a domestic water/livestock water supply point is shown in Figure A1.4.

An alternative system designed primarily for garden water supplies is shown in Photograph A1.3. In this design a bucket for clean water can be fitted under the Rower pump or without a bucket in place water discharges directly into a sub-surface sump. As there is no rise between the sump and the garden at this particular installation, a second Rower pump which is mounted beside the water storage tank is used to draw water for irrigation.

Photograph A1.3. Clean water/garden water supply

Another alternative arrangement is shown in Photograph A1.4 with a Rower and Joma pump combination to deliver water to a garden more than 10 metres above the Mtshelele River, Gwanda District, Matabeleland South, Zimbabwe. A diagram of this set up is shown in Figure A1.1.

Photograph A1.4. Rower and Joma Pump combination

A2

Useful contacts

IN THIS APPENDIX:
- Practitioners, Commercial, NGO and individual enthusiasts
- Equipment, suppliers
- Costs

The following is a list of some individuals, organisations and commercial companies that have experience and an interest either directly in sand-abstraction or in an allied aspect and are prepared to offer assistance in their particular field.

Practitioners

1. Dabane Trust has been developing small-scale sand-abstraction systems for some 15 years and has installed more than 100 mainly well-point systems in the remote rural areas of Zimbabwe. They are keen to promote and develop sand-abstraction systems and operate a cost recovery training programme for NGO staff in site identification and equipment installation. A 20 minute DVD 'Water from Sand Rivers' that demonstrates sand-abstraction technology and the work of the organization is available on request from Dabane Trust for US$ 5.00 +P&P.

   info@dabane.co.zw
   www.dabane.co.uk

2. Erik Nissen-Petersen is a well-established water conservationist with considerable experience of water harvesting systems and the development of water catchment systems including sand-abstraction and sand dams in Kenya. He has produced a range of 8 handbooks which have recently been updated and include:

   - Water for rural communities
   - Water from rock outcrops

174

- Water from dry riverbeds
- Water from roads
- Water from roofs
- Water from small dams
- Water surveys and designs
- Water projects by rural builders

Each manual is available free and can be downloaded from his website. He operates a commercial company, ASAL Consultants Ltd, PO Box 739, Sarit, 00606, Nairobi, Kenya.

asal@wananchi.com
asalconsultants@yahoo.com
www.waterforaridland.com

3. Richard Cansdale of SWS Filtration has extensive knowledge and experience of well-point and infiltration gallery design and installation gained over some 30 years work in Nigeria, Ghana, Tanzania, Madagascar and the Bahamas – as well as the United Kingdom and other countries in Europe. He has also developed the Rower pump and a very effective small-scale well-point. He has recently developed an efficient and durable direct action handpump the Canzee pump and more recently the Can-Lift Multi-valve handpump, which are both suitable for use on sand-abstraction wells.

richard@swsfilt.co.uk
http://www.swsfilt.co.uk/index.htm

4. Vernon Gibberd has some 40 years experience of hafir construction in Botswana and South Africa and is particularly interested in intensive vegetable production, where the size of the irrigated vegetable beds is matched to the capacity of the hafir.

vgibberd@iafrica.com

5. WETT (The Sustainable Water Extraction Technology Trust) is interested in providing assistance to extend the use of sand-abstraction into areas where it has not formerly been used. It is involved in research into areas that might have a potential and is keen to make contact with individuals and organisations interested in establishing sand-abstraction or the development of alternate water supplies.

s.w.hussey@ecoweb.co.zw
mans-ce0@wpmail.paisley.ac.uk

6. RIIC (Rural Industries Innovation Centre), Kanye, Botswana, have experience in lateral slotting uPVC pipes for use as infiltration gallery piping. They have also experimented with well-points that incorporate non-return valves for installation in caisson abstraction systems and have installed several sand-abstraction systems in Eastern and Northern Botswana. A report entitled 'Sand River Water Abstraction Scheme' has been produced by Ephraim Kgwarae.

ekgwarae@ripco.co.bw

7. Fred Dungan manages a useful web site; An Inexpensive Do-It-Yourself Water Well. Whilst not drawing water from a sand river his experience of driving a well-point to a satisfactory depth into a sand/gravelbed in California may well be of interest and use to anyone about to try.

http://www.fdungan.com/well.htm

8. Geomeasure Services, Durban, South Africa have an interesting web site indicating that they have extensive experience in sand-abstraction and community water supply work.

info@geomeasuregroup.co.za
www.geomeasuregroup.co.za

Equipment suppliers

Commercial companies that manufacture well-points, some of which are particularly suitable for sand-abstraction use.

1. Boode manufacture a wide range of screens from large-scale infiltration galleries to small-scale well-points. Of particular interest is a small ceramic screen that is suitable for use in alluvium that is too fine for round aperture screens. Boode Water Well, Screen and Casing Systems, Zevnhuizen, Netherlands.

www.**boode**.com

2. Johnson Screens have extensive experience in well-screen technology and have produced a comprehensive book that covers all aspects of water drilling and screen development, (Groundwater and Wells: A comprehensive study of groundwater and the technologies used to locate, extract, treat and protect this resource, written by Fletcher G. Driscoll, Johnson Filtration Systems Inc., St. Paul, Minnesota 55112, USA, ISBN 0-9616456-0-1). The company markets stainless steel taper, wire wound, self-jetting well-points. It is probably more experienced in large-scale schemes and supplied the well-points to an irrigation scheme

in south west Zimbabwe that has a potential to irrigate 1,200ha from a sand-abstraction water source on the Save River.

www.johnsonscreens.com

3. Soloflo, South Africa market a tapering uPVC, radially slotted screen that has been used extensively in sand-abstraction installations in southern Africa.

info@soloflo.co.za
http://www.soloflo.com/home.htm

4. SWS Filtration manufacture and sell complete units, components and spares of well-points, infiltration galleries, Rower pumps and direct action pumps suitable for small-scale community water supplies.

richard@swsfilt.co.uk

5. Kaytech market a range of synthetic geotextiles with varying rates of thickness and permeability that are suitable for covering well-points with large diameter apertures or slots to make them more suitable for installation in very fine sediments.

http://www.kaytech.co.za/

A web search indicates that the following companies manufacture well-points

6. Big Eastern Wetlands

http://www.bigeastern.com/eotp/ep_mars.htm

7. Big Foot Manufacturing – Slotted PVC well-screens

http://www.bigfootmfg.com/slotted;screens.html

8. Chemdrex Chemicals – Water well-screens

http://www.chemdrex.com.au/screens.htm

9. Dean Bennett Supply Company – Well-screens

http://www.deanbennett.com.sand-stopper-screens.htm

10. Eijkelkamp

http://www.barlofco.co.za/solutions/sols05.htm

11. Roscoe Moss

http://www.roscoemoss.com/well_casing;screen.html

12. Con-slot

http://www.carbisfiltration.co.uk/

Appendix 2

Dabane Trust pump costs

Simple suction pump to draw from a depth of 4 to 5 metres with no delivery head. The pump costs in the table below are those of the pump in its most basic form as described in Appendix 1 and shown in Figure 11.4. The pump can also be assembled in a more elaborate form that is more suitable for a clean water supply as shown in Figure 7.1. Foot valves and piston bodies can also be purchased from manufacturer/suppliers such as SWS Filtration.

Table A2.1. Cost of a Rower pump – made in Zimbabwe from locally available materials at US dollar prices (May 2007)

		Materials	Unit of measure	Qty	Unit cost (US$)	Total cost US$
1	Pump body	Pump cylinder (63mm class 16 rigid uPVC pipe)	m	1.66	9.87	16.38
2		Connection to suction pipe (63mm VSP)	63mm	1	5.23	5.23
3	Foot valve	Foot valve (uPVC sheet; 1000x595x10mm)	m2	0.004	26.40	0.11
4		3mm x 10mm self tapping screw	each	1	0.11	0.11
5	Piston body	Piston body (uPVC sheet; 1000x595x10mm)	m2	0.016	26.40	0.42
6		Cup seals	each	4	0.98	3.92
7	Pump handle	Pump rod (10mm bright steel)	m	1.5	2.09	3.14
8		Pump rod handle (19mm furniture tube)	m	0.3	3.07	0.92
9		Hex nut	10mm	1	0.14	0.14
10		Nyloc nut	10mm	1	0.27	0.27
11		Flat washers	10mm	1	0.05	0.05
9	Fabrication materials	Solvent cement (500 mls)	each	0.08	1.60	0.13
10		Emery tape (medium)	roll	0.005	36.84	0.18
11		Hacksaw blades (18 tooth)	each	0.02	0.65	0.01
12		Hacksaw blades (24 tooth)	each	0.02	0.65	0.01
12	Production costs	Procurement costs	hrs	0.5	1.20	0.60
13		Manufacturing costs	hrs	6	2.27	13.62
14		Fitting materials and depreciation on Tools	% of materials	3.33%	22.99	0.77
					Total	**$46.01**

Note: 63mm VSP - a PVC fitting with a 2inch (50mm) male water pipe thread which is cemented to the pump body to connect to the supply pipe from the well-point.

Dabane Trust well-point costs

A simple well-point fabricated from 40mm class 10 uPVC pipe which can be either dug into river channel sediment in a shallow excavation or, where possible, driven to a depth of 3 to 5 metres. The well-point has a sacrificial tip with 'wings' to prevent it being extracted from the sediment when the driving tube is withdrawn. A representation of the well-point is shown in Figure 11.3. The spreadsheet used in the design of the well-point is shown in Appendix 1.

		Materials	Unit of measure	Qty	Unit cost (US$)	Total cost US$
Table A2.2. Cost of a 40mm diameter round aperture well-point (May 2007)						
1	Tube	Well-point tube (40mm class 10 rigid uPVC pipe)	m	0.5	2.84	1.42
2	Sacrificial tip	Galvanised steel water pipe (1.5" - 40mm)	m	0.15	22.47	3.37
3		Galvanised steel water pipe (2" - 50mm)	m	0.03	29.62	0.89
4		Flat bar (40 x 4.5mm)	m	0.40	17.37	6.95
5		Wire nail (150mm)	kg	0.02	6.81	0.14
6	Connection fittings	MIFP	40mm	1	5.17	5.17
7		Swage coupling (Polypipe adaptor)	40mm	1	3.53	3.53
8		Jubilee clip (50mm)	each	2	0.28	0.56
9	Fabrication materials	Solvent cement (500 mls)	each	0.04	1.60	0.06
10		Emery tape (medium)	roll	0.0025	36.84	0.09
11		Hacksaw blades (18 tooth)	each	0.04	0.65	0.03
12		Hacksaw blades (24 tooth)	each	0.04	0.65	0.03
13	Production costs	Procurement costs	hrs	0.5	1.20	0.60
14		Manufacturing costs	hrs	3.5	2.27	7.95
15		Fitting materials & depreciation on tools	% of materials	2.5%	30.78	0.77
					Total	**$31.55**

Note: 40mm MIFP - a PVC fitting with a female 1 1/2 inch (40mm) water pipe thread which is cemented to the well-point tube.
40mm swage coupling - a plastic fitting which fits into the pipe thread of the MIFP and connects to 40mm LPDE (low density polyethylene) pipe.
50mm jubilee clip - a fastener to ensure an airtight fit between the swage coupling and the LDPE pipe, (a 50mm clip is easier to fit on a 40mm pipe than a 40mm).
Due to varying material and variable lengths, diameter and class of piping, costs of connecting pipes between the well-point and rower pump are not included.

A3

Global overview

Appendix 3

IN THIS APPENDIX:
- Regions, countries and localities where sand-abstraction systems are in use and where the possibility exists for small-scale sand-abstraction technology
- Review of further localities where sand-abstraction may not be used but where the possibility may exist to establish developed sand-abstraction systems

Sand-abstraction in the manner and systems described has been primarily developed in southern Africa although the technology is in widespread use in several countries and in particular in North America where it is used in collector wells and driven well-points. Systems generally similar to sand-abstraction are also used in streambed abstraction in perennial rivers in temperate zones and include sea water intakes through infiltration galleries that are installed into beach sand. The abstraction technology is thus well established and in one way or another sand-abstraction is used almost anywhere on the globe that there is free moving water in sediment. However, it is dryland areas to which sand-abstraction is particularly suited.

Approximately one third of the world described as arid or semi-arid lies between latitudes 30° north and 30° south of the equator. On the basis of climate, dryland regions occupy 36% of the earth's land surface with many of the countries within the region categorized as water deficit. The most extensive arid area of the world is the desert region of the Sahara and Sahel that stretches across north Africa. Other desert areas in the region are the Danakil which occurs in Eritrea and northern Ethiopia, the Ogaden in Somalia and south east Ethiopia, the Chalbi in northern Kenya and the Didi Galgalu desert in eastern Kenya. In southern Africa there are the Kalahari and the Namib Deserts. In the Middle East the desert regions are the Arabian Desert, the Indo-Iranian deserts of Iran, Afghanistan and Pakistan and the Thar Desert of India.

The desert regions of central Asia primarily occur in Turkmenistan, Uzbekistan, Kazakhstan and Tibet together with the Taklimakan and Gobi deserts of China. The desert regions of South America are the Patagonia and Atacama Deserts. Much of the continent of Australia is designated as desert as are parts of the south east of North America. Whilst sand-abstraction is only possible at a few localities in the arid areas of deserts there are generally extensive possibilities in the semi-arid areas of the desert margins.

Figure A3.1 indicates global precipitation and the regions that are most likely to be suitable for small-scale sand-abstraction development.

Documented evidence exists of developed sand-abstraction systems for community, small-scale irrigation, commercial agriculture and mining use in the dryland areas of Zimbabwe, Botswana, Namibia, Swaziland and South Africa. A wide range of abstraction technology has been used in these countries from the basic, small-scale hand operated to sophisticated, large high-tech automated schemes. Reliable reports of either developed or traditional sand-abstraction systems have also been received from south west Zambia (Barotseland), northern and western Kenya, Somaliland, southern and western Sudan, northern Nigeria and isolated parts of Morocco. The schemes have been mainly small-scale and for the benefit of rural communities.

There is also documented evidence of the seasonal use of riverbed sand wells in India in the Kerala, Ragistan and Orissa States. Although these wells are generally not perennial as the riverbed alluvium does not accrue to a depth sufficient to retain water for year round use there is greater opportunity for water supplies from tube-wells installed in alluvial riverbanks, sand or gravelbeds. Where appropriate tube-well technology is used extensively throughout Pakistan, India and Bangladesh. Temporary wells are also dug into the dry rocky beds of fast flowing rivers in arid or semi-arid mountainous countries such as Tibet, Nepal and Mongolia, as well as into seasonal riverbeds in the rural areas of western China and the former Soviet Republics of Kazakhstan, Turkmenistan and Uzbekistan. In the Andes nations of Bolivia and Peru the gradients of riverbeds are typically high. Consequently the sediment is very coarse with high rates of transport so that water abstraction is more likely to be from riverbed intakes than sand-abstraction. Isolated schemes have been reported in New Mexico and Arizona in the USA where there are seasonal rivers. However the rivers there generally have an insufficient depth of river channel sediment for reliable sand-abstraction use.

Appendix 3

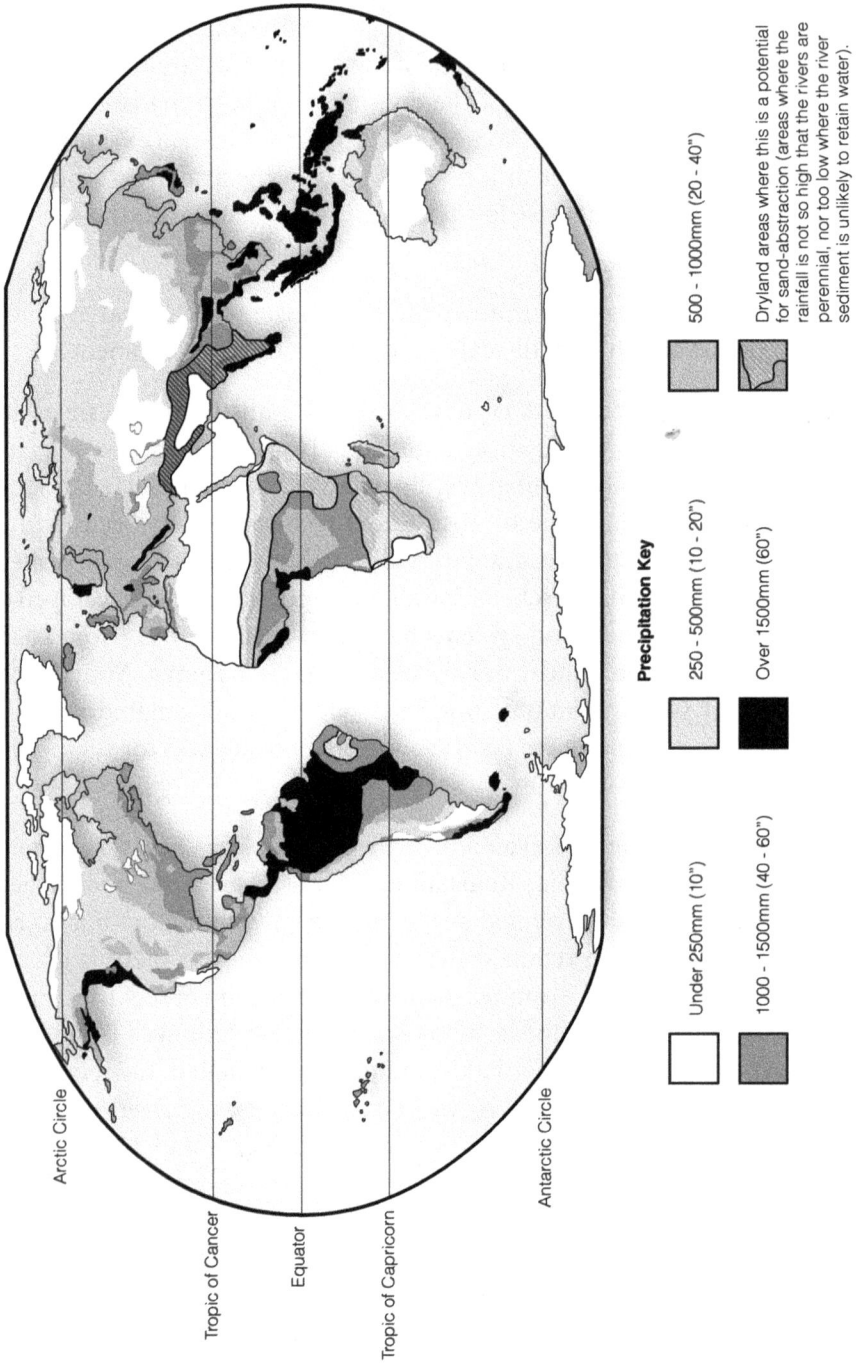

Figure A3.1. Dryland regions that have a potential for sand-abstraction

Other areas where there are possible applications for sand-abstraction related systems are north east Brazil, where run-off water harvesting from seasonal river flow is directed into unlined pits to recharge riverbank aquifers. The Middle East and parts of the Indian sub-continent have also established water harvesting traditions. Research and documented reports indicate possibilities in parts of other countries in Latin America.

Apart from well-points and tube-wells, infiltration galleries are widely used in Iraq, Iran and Afghanistan as well as in Algeria, Northern Mexico, California and Hawaii. They are also widely used in Oceania, particularly Tonga but also in Samoa and Fiji where they are used to abstract the islands' shallow groundwater supplies and to reduce the risk of excessive saltwater intrusion. Infiltration gallery systems installed in the sand or gravelbeds below perennial river systems is an established practice in both the United States and the United Kingdom.

Sand 'spears' are used to abstract shallow groundwater from sand and gravelbeds in and around Cape Town, South Africa as well as parts of West Australia and Queensland in Australia and in Ohio, Iowa, Michigan, Wisconsin, Minnesota, New York State, Georgia and Florida in the United States.

Many of the incidents recorded are traditional open wells which are dug into dry streambeds. With suitable site identification and possible development and selection of an appropriate abstraction technology there is ample opportunity for greater utilisation of the water reserves in sand rivers, sand and gravelbeds.

Appendix 3

A4

Glossary

Appendix 4

Adsorption	A process of adhesion to the surface of a material.
Alluvium	Soil or sediments deposited by a river or other running water comprising gravel, sand, silt and mud.
Aeolian sand	Material which has been transported by the wind and as a consequence is worn and deposited as small, rounded particles.
Aquifer	A formation of rock or sediment that contains quantities of water that can be released in usable quantities.
Aquitard	A formation of rock or sediment with a low permeability that stores groundwater but delays its flow elsewhere.
Arid	Relates to climates or regions with an average annual rainfall of less than 200mm.
Biofouling	Bacterial slime of algae and micro organisms which grows on immersed equipment such as well-points and pipe work. Excessive accumulation creates blockages of screen apertures and pipe work.
Caisson	A concrete or brick structure on the bed of a river constructed for abstracting water.

Clasts	Clastic sedimentary rocks are rocks composed predominantly of broken pieces or 'clasts' of older weathered and eroded rocks.
Collector well	A vertical well shaft incorporating one or more horizontal screens that allows groundwater to infiltrate from riverbed sediment, the base of the river channel or from a gravel or sand bed.
Compaction	The process of granular material becoming more closely packed together.
Confined aquifer	An aquifer that is bounded above and below by formations of lower permeability. The aquifer itself is not in direct connection with the atmosphere and does not have a free water-table.
Contaminant	A chemical or biological suspension that is detrimental to water quality and reduces its usability for drinking, food preparation or washing.
Dryland	Land that may have vegetation suitable for grazing livestock but is too arid for crop farming.
Endogenous river	A regularly flowing river or stream that originates within arid lands. Such rivers often do not reach the sea but drain into inland basins where the water evaporates and is lost in the ground.
Ephemeral river	A stream or river which does not flow at all times of the year.
Erosion	Wearing away of rock and land surface largely by the actions of material carried by water or wind.
Evaporation	The loss of water due to a change from liquid to vapour phases, made worse by high temperatures and wind.

Appendix 4

Evapo-transpiration	The total loss of moisture from the soil and open water through evaporation and by transpiration from growing plants in the form of water vapour.
Exogenous river	A perennial river flowing through a dryland area with a source outside the arid zone.
Flood plain	Flat land alongside a river that consists of alluvium deposited by the river when in flood.
Groundwater	Water that occurs beneath the land surface and which fills the voids of the alluvium, soil, or rock formation in which it is situated.
Gravelbed	A deposit of rounded stones between 2mm and 80mm diameter that were formed by the action of moving water, usually mixed with finer materials such as sand or clay and typically the surface will be vegetated.
Hafir	A lined or unlined artificial reservoir collecting water from a river channel or rainfall from surface run-off.
Headworks	Infrastructure around a pump, generally concrete work, intended to keep the pump surrounds clean and drained.
Hydraulic head	Potential energy contained in a mass of water due to differences in elevation and atmospheric pressure.
Infiltration	The flow of water downward from the land surface into and through the upper soil layers.
Infiltration gallery	One or more horizontal screens placed adjacent to or directly beneath a shallow source of water to increase the supply.

Appendix 4

Jetting	A process of installing a well-point into sediment using a jet of water.
Manifold	A chamber with one or more inlets that reduces the velocity of water through a supply system.
Mineral salts	Salts released from rocks that are dissolved in water. Fast draining aquifers tend to contain few salts, slow draining aquifers may be more saline.
Offset *(false well)*	A well adjacent to a river with water artificially supplied from river alluvium.
Open surface	A water surface open to evaporation.
Paleo river channel *(fossil riverbed)*	A river channel that occurred at a time when the climate of a region was wetter than at present and no longer has a flow of water.
Permeability	A measure of the ability of rocks or sediments to allow the flow of water, measured in metres per unit time.
Perched aquifer	An aquifer that is not connected with the main body of groundwater due to an underlying layer of impermeable material.
Perennial river	A stream or river with continuous flow.
Persian Wheel	A vertical wheel with buckets for lifting water from a depth approximately the radius of the wheel, usually animal-powered.
Porosity	The ratio of the voids or open spaces in alluvium (and rocks) to the total volume of the alluvium or rock mass.
Potable water	Water of sufficient quality to serve as drinking water that does not contain disease producing vectors or pathogens and whose chemistry does not cause long-term health problems.

Appendix 4

Qanat *(karez or foggara)*	An underground tunnel constructed into a hillside to access an aquifer. The tunnels gently rise to the aquifer to allow the water to drain under the influence of gravity.
Run-off	Water moving over a land surface which is not absorbed into the soil.
Safe water	Water that is not harmful for human beings or contaminated to the extent of being unhealthy.
Sand-abstraction	The process of taking water from the saturated sediment of sand rivers.
Sandbed	A layer of sediment whose grain size is between 0,06mm and 2mm (finer than a gravel bed).
Sand well *(scoop well)*	A seasonal unlined well excavated in river channel sediment to access saturated sediment.
Saturated sediment	Sediment in which all pores, voids and interconnected openings are filled with water.
Seasonal river	River or stream that flows only during and following rainfall and is dry at all other times.
Sediment	Layers of coarse to fine grained rock particles deposited by flowing water or by wind action.
Seepage	A diffuse flow of water from an aquifer.
Self jetting well-point	A well-point incorporating a valve to allow direct installation by jetting. When pumping commences the valve closes forcing water to enter the well-point through a screen.
Semi-arid	Relates to climates or regions with an average annual rainfall of less than 600 mm.

Appendix 4

Specific yield	The ratio of the volume of water in a soil or rock, that will flow by gravity drainage, to the total volume of the material.

Shadoof	A hand device used to raise water by way of a counter-balanced pole, with a bucket at one end and a weight on the other.

Transmissivity	A measure of the volume of water that can move horizontally through the entire saturated thickness of an aquifer, measured in metres squared per unit time and used to determine the potential yield of a well or well-point.

Unconfined aquifer	An aquifer which is not bounded on top by an aquitard, the upper surface of which is the water-table.

Wadi	A dry riverbed in an arid zone that contains water only during times of heavy rain. As flow is often the result of an intense localized storm a wadi typically has no source or outlet.

Water-table	Level in the ground below which rock strata are saturated with water.

Weathering	Breakdown of rocks resulting from the action of wind, rain, temperature change, plants and other organisms.

Well-point	A pipe or screen with openings large enough to allow water to enter and small enough to exclude most of the water-bearing sediment. The size of openings in the well-point is determined by analysis of the size of particles in the alluvium.

Well-screen	A holed or slotted mechanism for separating water from sediment, see well-point.

Appendix 4

A5

Further reading

Hydrology

- British Soil Classification System – BS 5930
  – British Soil Classification System for Engineering
- Field Hydrology – R. Brassington – John Wiley & Sons,
  ISBN 0-471-93205-1
- Field Hydrology in Tropical Countries – Henry Gunston –
  Intermediate Technology Publications, ISBN 1 85339 427 0
- Ground Water – H.M. Raghunath – Wiley Eastern Limited –
  ISBN 0 85226 298 1
- Groundwater and Wells – Fletcher G Driscoll – Johnson Filtration
  Systems Inc, ISBN 0-9616456-0-1
- Groundwater Assessment, Development and Management –
  K R Karanth – Tata, McGraw-Hill Publishing Company
- Hydrology, the Field Guide to Water Wells and Boreholes –
  L Clark – John Wiley & Sons, ISBN 0-471-93211-6
- Introducing Groundwater – Michael Price – Chapman & Hall,
  ISBN 0 412 48500 1
- Rural and Urban Hydrology – M.G. Mansell - Thomas Telford,
  ISBN 0 7277 3230 7
- Tropical Residual Soils – PG Fookes – Geological Society, London
- The Storage of Water in Sand – O. Wipplinger. This book published
  in 1958 is now out of print, however it provides an interesting
  academic perspective of early research into sand-abstraction
  and copies are sometimes available in university libraries
- Water Resources in the Arid Realm – C Agnew and E Anderson –
  Routledge

Rural water supplies

- Alternative Irrigation – the promise of runoff Agriculture – C.J. Barrow, ISBN 185383 4963
- Productive Water Points in Dryland Areas – Guidelines on integrated planning for rural water supply – Chris Lovell – Practical Action Publishing, ISBN 1 85339 516 1
- Running water, more technical briefs on health, water and sanitation – Edited by Rod Shaw – Intermediate Technology Publications 1999
- Rural Water Supplies and Sanitation – Peter Morgan – Macmillian Education Ltd, ISBN 0-333-48569-6
- Small-scale Water Supply – Brian Skinner – Practical Action Publishing, ISBN 1 85339 540 4
- Water for rural communities – Erik Nissen-Petersen, Birgit Madsen, Munguti Katui-Katua – DANIDA – 2006 – ASAL consultants ltd., PO Box 739, Sarit 00606, Nairobi, Kenya – cmts2001@mitsuminet.com cmts2001@hotmail.com
- Water from dry riverbeds – Erik Nissen-Petersen – DANIDA – 2006 – Community management and training services ltd., PO Box 292 – 00206, Kiserian, Kenya – asal@wananchi.com salconsultants@yahoo.com
- WATER in Southern Africa – SADC – Environment and land management sector co-ordination unit, ISBN 0-7974-1672-2
- Water Resources and Agricultural Development in the Tropics: a Handbook – C Barrow – Longmans Scientific & Technical

Pumps and abstraction systems

- Community water supply – the handpump option – Saul Arlosoroff, Gerhard
- Handpumps – Issues and concepts in rural water supply programmes – Technical Paper No 25 – IRC International Water and Sanitation Centre, ISBN 90-6687-010-9
- How to Make and Use the Treadle Irrigation Pump – Carl Bielenberg and Hugh Allen – Intermediate Technology Publications, ISBN 1 85339 312 6

Appendix 5

- Ranney Wells – L Christensen – http://www.laynechristensen.com/ranney_group.html
- Rural Water Supply in Africa, Building blocks for handpump sustainability – Peter Harvey and Bob Reed – WEDC 2004
- Water from Dry Riverbeds – Erik Nissen-Petersen – Danish International Development Assistance – www.waterforaridland.com
- Water-pumping Devices – Peter Fraenkel – Intermediate Technology Publications, ISBN 1 85339 346 0

Social aspects

- Community Water Development – selected and edited by Charles Kerr – Intermediate Technology Publications, ISBN 0 94668 823 0
- Developing and Managing Community Water Supplies – Jan Davis and Gerry Garvey, with Michael Wood – Development Guidelines No 8, OXFAM, ISBN 0 85598 193 8
- Dying Wisdom Rise, Fall and Potential of India's Traditional Water Harvesting Systems – A Narain – Centre for Science and Environment, New Delphi
- The Human Factor in Community Work – TR Batten and M Batten – Oxford University Press.

Appendix 5

Index

www.ingramcontent.com/pod-product-compliance
Lightning Source LLC
Chambersburg PA
CBHW080249030426
42334CB00023BA/2745